Cats' X. Y. Z.

Beverley Nichols, with Leo, at Sudbrook Cottage. Courtesy of the Bryan Connon Collection.

BEVERLEY NICHOLS'

Cats'
X. Y. Z.

With a foreword by
Juliet Clutton-Brock

Timber Press
Portland • Cambridge

Photograph of Beverley Nichols is the property of Bryan Connon, reproduced by permission

Drawings by Derrick Sayer

First published in 1961 by Jonathan Cape

Foreword copyright © 2003 by Timber Press, Inc.

Timber Press, Inc.
The Haseltine Building
133 S.W. Second Avenue, Suite 450
Portland, Oregon 97204-3527, U.S.A.

Timber Press
2 Station Road
Swavesey
Cambridge CB4 5QJ, U.K.

Printed through Colorcraft Ltd., Hong Kong

Library of Congress Cataloging-in-Publication Data

Nichols, Beverley, 1898–1983
   [Cats' X. Y. Z.]
   Beverley Nichols' cats' X. Y. Z. / with a foreword by Juliet Clutton-Brock.
     p. cm.
   Originally published: Cats' X. Y. Z. : Jonathan Cape, 1961.
   ISBN 0-88192-594-2
   1. Cats. I. Title: Cats' X. Y. Z. II. Title.
  SF442 .N5 2003
  636.8—dc21

                                           2003047308

A catalogue record for this book is also available from the British Library.

Contents

Foreword

In his *Cats' X. Y. Z.*, Beverley Nichols continues his enchanting description of the lives of 'Four', 'Five' and Oscar. Their loves and hates, their purring times and their moments of discomfort are recounted and intermingled with innumerable anecdotes about life in his idyllic country house and garden. Written in the early post-war years, when resources in England were still in short supply, life could nonetheless be full of joy for cats and people.

Beverley Nichols had no problem with the certain knowledge that his cats were as self-aware as he was, and he found every opportunity in his writing to express his horror of cruelty and his distaste for the circuses and zoos of his time. He would have had no patience with the small but influential school of so-called behaviourism that had a following among some biologists in the 1950s. They promoted the theory that animal behaviour is purely a response to physiological or hormonal reactions to external stimuli, and they threw scorn on the work of Konrad Lorenz as anthropomorphic. Some scientists even tried to preach that animals do not feel pain in the way that humans do.

Today, these views are obsolete. Animal behaviour and animal welfare are studied as sciences, and a pet behaviour counsellor can be called upon to sort out any emotional or psychological difficulty, such as separation anxiety, from which your pet may suffer. Beverley Nichols would probably have approved but he would have needed no such help.

Beverley Nichols' Cats' A. B. C. and *Cats' X. Y. Z.* are books to dip into for relaxation after a busy day. But they are also books to read right through, time and again, to savour their charm and wisdom.

JULIET CLUTTON-BROCK, B.SC., PH.D, D.SC., F.Z.S., F.S.A.
In Cat World, *Desmond Morris described Dr Clutton-Brock as 'the world's greatest authority on the history of domestic animals'*

THE CATS' X.Y.Z.

BEVERLEY NICHOLS

has written the following books on cats, and
gardens in which cats figure prominently

Down the Garden Path, 1932
A Thatched Roof, 1933
A Village in a Valley, 1934
Green Grows the City, 1939
Merry Hall, 1951
Laughter on the Stairs, 1953
Beverley Nichols' Cat Book [1955]
Sunlight on the Lawn, 1956
Beverley Nichols' Cats' A. B. C., 1960
Beverley Nichols' Cats' X. Y. Z., 1961
Foreword to Jan Styczynski's *Cats in Camera*, 1962
Garden Open Today, 1963
Garden Open Tomorrow, 1968
Foreword to Orbis's *All About Cats*, 1975

BEVERLEY NICHOLS'

Cats'
X.Y.Z.

Illustrated by Derrick Sayer

JONATHAN CAPE
THIRTY BEDFORD SQUARE · LONDON

FIRST PUBLISHED 1961

TEXT © 1961 BY BEVERLEY NICHOLS

DRAWINGS © 1961 BY JONATHAN CAPE LTD

SET AND PRINTED IN GREAT BRITAIN BY
BALDING & MANSELL, LONDON AND WISBECH
BOUND BY A. W. BAIN & CO. LTD, LONDON

Author's Note

The title of this little book does not imply that its author imagines himself to have said the last word about cats; it is merely a phrase of convenience, which will tell those who were mildly diverted by my *A.B.C.* what they may expect in the following pages. Equally, it will warn those who were fiercely repelled by the *A.B.C.*—the fanatical anti-felines—to give the present volume a wide berth.

Nobody will ever say the last word about cats, the most elegant and the most mysterious of God's creatures. The more intimately one seems to know them, the less predictable their behaviour. Although the feline cast of the *X.Y.Z.* is identical with that of the *A.B.C.*—'Four', 'Five' and Oscar having been mercifully preserved through the past year—hardly a day has passed in which they have not revealed new and unexpected facets of their characters. 'Four', as will be observed, has greatly enlarged and extended his wide range of dramatic roles; 'Five' has become at once more plump and more Sphinx-like; while Oscar . . . however, Oscar is best left to speak for himself. In any case, it would be useless to try to stop him.

A word about the expressions 'F' and 'non-F', which recur fairly frequently. As I explained in the *A.B.C.*, they are intended to describe persons who are basically feline or non-feline by nature. Thus, Chopin was F, Bach non-F. Rubens was F, Rembrandt non-F. And so forth. These classifications are not to be taken as a measure of greatness, nor of virtue. It is simply a question of how one is born.

Perhaps I can explain it most clearly by observing that there are even F dogs. Most bulldogs are distinctly F, and so are large numbers of poodles, many Pekinese, and almost all sheep dogs. On the other hand I have yet to meet a fox-terrier who was F, or a dachshund. The least F dog, of course, is the corgi. This underlines the curious circumstance that Royalty itself, by and large, tends to be firmly non-F—a fact which does not prevent one from being a loyal subject.   B. (F) N.

Acknowledgments

My thanks are due to the following for permission to quote the verses included in this book: the Trustees of the Hardy Estate and Macmillan & Co. Ltd for the lines from 'Last Words to a Dumb Friend' from *The Collected Poems of Thomas Hardy*; The Bodley Head Ltd for the lines from *The Sphinx* by Oscar Wilde; and Chapman and Grimes, Inc., Boston, U.S.A., for the verses 'Wind is a cat' by Ethel Romig Fuller and 'I have no pets to hold my heart' by Helen Maring, both from their publication *Sophisti-Cats*, compiled and edited by Lynn Hamilton.

AUTUMN

There had been a sharp frost in the night, the first of the season, and when I went out into the garden after breakfast the little golden acacia at the far end of the lawn was standing in a circle of fallen yellow leaves, like a young girl who had just stepped out of a silken dress. Near by, the liquidambers were so thickly hung with frosted cobwebs that their twigs seemed to be *diamanté*, and I remember thinking that they were really rather overdressed . . . all those jewels at so early an hour. (Which reminds me of a very rich acquaintance whom I once surprised in the herbaceous border, pulling up groundsel, which of course is the nicest weed to pull up. She was wearing a smock of expensive simplicity and a beautiful pearl necklace. I made some remark about the necklace and she replied, quite casually and with no trace of affectation, 'Oh . . . these are my gardening pearls.' In spite of this she is an agreeable woman, and fundamentally F[1].)

But we were talking of autumn. There I was, standing on the lawn, not only looking but listening, to one of the most magical echoes in the whole symphony of nature, the sound of falling leaves. They were falling from the branches of the old walnut tree that stretched its gnarled branches over the outbuildings, and the morning was so hushed that one heard each leaf distinctly as it fell, sighing and fluttering through the misty air. It would be pleasant, I thought, if we could all leave the world in so graceful a fashion; at one moment high up in the branches of an old tree, and then—a sudden feeling of fatigue, a swift farewell and a gentle parting,

[1] A note on the correct interpretation of Fness and non-Fness will be found in the foreword, in case it has escaped your attention.

9

knowing, as we left the parent branch, that even now, though a new life awaited us, it would be a life of growth and service.

And then, the silence was broken by a cough behind me. I looked round and saw 'Four', the eldest of my three cats. He was sitting on the yellow leaves of the acacia, and he looked very black, very cold, and very pathetic. He coughed again.

Now it must be explained that 'Four', in case this is the first time that you have met him, is the Cat Who Does the Act. A fuller interpretation of this title will be found under 'Jealousy'. For the moment it is enough to say that at a very early age 'Four' decided that he would be most likely to obtain a lion's share of the good things of life if he adopted a role in which he appeared to be persecuted and maltreated. He has never, to my knowledge, received even the mildest of slaps, but if he is not getting his own way in every respect he will immediately register an expression of terror, and retreat with such alarm and dismay that anybody witnessing this little drama immediately leaps to the conclusion that I am a cat-beater.

Coughing is part of the Act. It is usually employed if the fish is not served precisely to his liking. 'Four' bends over the plate, sniffs, turns round, and then—always provided that he has an audience—goes straight into the Act with a positive Mimi of a cough. The assumption, of course, is that he is a poor, neglected creature, rapidly heading for a decline, whose demise can only be averted by a swiftly opened tin of tongue. It is all very professionally timed and executed, and the only reason it is not quite heart-rending is that 'Four', like many other Mimis whom one has seen ex-piring in Act Four of *La Bohème*, is exceedingly plump.

Still, one never knew. 'Four' *might* have a real cough. After all, he was getting on, like others who shall be nameless. There had been a worry-ing week, three years ago, when he had bronchitis. I bent down, picked him up, and gently felt the tip of his nose. Oh dear . . . it was hot. And 'Four' usually has a nose as cold as an icicle.

So here we went again. Away from the falling leaves, away from the peace of the garden, and back to the house with 'Four' snuggling in our arms, to seek out Gaskin, who would know what to do.

BACKWATER

Without any great effort on our part, the stage of this little revue seems to have set itself—the high-walled garden adrift with falling leaves. And two of the main characters have introduced themselves—'Four', the eldest of our feline trio, and Gaskin, the factotum and friend of many years. Now that 'Four' is safely in Gaskin's arms—'I knew that this would happen; he *will* sit right in the stove in the draught of the cat-door'—we can briefly introduce the two other principal players, 'Five' and Oscar.

Both are tabbies, but there the resemblance ends. 'Five,' who does not eat excessively, is round and very plump; Oscar, who eats like a horse, remains lean and lanky. 'Five', in spite of his plumpness, is something of a cynic, and plays 'hard to get'. This, I suspect, is due to the fact that when he was a baby he was chased all over the house by a Pekinese and ended up by jumping on to the lawn from a high window . . . one of those moments in one's life one would prefer to forget. (Whenever I hear people saying 'Of course, cats can fall from *any* height without hurting themselves' I feel like retorting 'Quite. And if a woman is silly enough you can pour boiling oil down her neck without her even noticing it.')

Where were we? Oh yes. . .'Five', and his cynicism. Oscar, on the other hand, has no trace of cynicism; he is a pushover, mentally and physically, for anybody who shows him affection. And since most of my friends are firmly F, he spends a great deal of his life flopping on to his back, with his front paws dangling, demanding chin-strokings and tummy-rubbings. And, in the case of exceptionally advanced Fs, reversed whisker-strokings.[1]

[1] A note on reversed whisker-stroking will be found in a later section. It demands a very high standard of technique, and may be compared, pianistically, with the cadenza in the eleventh section of Rachmaninoff's Paganini Variations. It should not be attempted by amateurs.

'Four', 'Five' and Oscar having made their brief bows, in their respective fashions, I should like to 'pan back', as I believe they say in the movie studios, and take a wider view, so that we may see our little house as though it were on a large-scale map, with the various neighbouring cats marked with a cross. However, since this section has already run to an inordinate length, let us move on.

My cottage is situated on Ham Common, in the county of Surrey, and perhaps some people might quarrel with the description of such a locality as a 'backwater'. They would point out that only three miles to the north is the flourishing county town of Richmond, through which the traffic pours to the sea-coast. And that three miles to the south is the equally flourishing county town of Kingston . . . to say nothing of the crowds that throng Hampton Court throughout the summer.

However, certain parts of England have a strange magic which might be described as a quality of withdrawal; they seem to turn into backwaters in their own right. And just as in the City of London you may suddenly step from the traffic's roar into a courtyard as hushed and tranquil as Magdalene College in the Long Vacation, so, in the neighbourhood of my cottage, you have only to walk a few yards to find yourself in the heart of the country.

I open the front door, sniff the sweet air, and the even sweeter lemon-verbena which flourishes by the porch. I turn to the left, past the cottages of my neighbours, which like my own were built in the year 1800 and look exactly like a setting for one of Jane Austen's novels. At the end of the row, an exquisite Queen Anne house looms into view, a fairy-tale house whose name is . . . but let us keep some mystery in these pages. I shall call it the Great House, and I shall name its charming young owners Lord and Lady X. And I shall indulge myself in dreams of future days when, as an extremely impoverished and decrepit author, I sit by a starveling fire, polishing my crutches, and Lady X knocks on the door with a bowl of soup.

These painful scenes have not yet materialized. Lady X has indeed knocked on the door, but the last time she did so it was to borrow a lemon from Gaskin because somebody had unexpectedly sent them a tin of caviar.

I want to linger for a few more moments in front of the Great House. It is all part of the feline setting; 'Four', 'Five', and Oscar often visit it, via the garden walls, though I do not think that as yet they have formally left their cards. Most days of my life I wander past it, on my way to the silver birch woods, and always I pause, peopling it with the ghosts who must still tenant it. Sometimes I think I see the pale frustrated face of Mrs Fitzherbert, staring out of one of the windows in the west wing, cursing the rain-swept common to which she had been banished when her fortunes were at their lowest ebb. But always I see the bent, shabby figure of Daniel Defoe, ambling his way across the lawn to vanish in the shadows of the giant cedars. For it was from the bricks of Defoe's little factory on the Thames that the Great House was built. The author of *Robinson Crusoe* was probably the first professional writer, and certainly not the last, who found it necessary to augment his income by taking jobs 'on the side'.

None of which, as you may well remind me, has anything to do with cats.

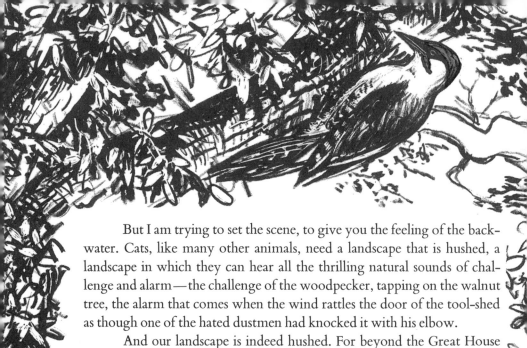

But I am trying to set the scene, to give you the feeling of the back-water. Cats, like many other animals, need a landscape that is hushed, a landscape in which they can hear all the thrilling natural sounds of challenge and alarm—the challenge of the woodpecker, tapping on the walnut tree, the alarm that comes when the wind rattles the door of the tool-shed as though one of the hated dustmen had knocked it with his elbow.

And our landscape is indeed hushed. For beyond the Great House the woods begin, my favourite kind of woods, all silver birch and bracken. And beyond the woods are the wide, rolling expanses of Richmond Park, with the wild deer playing. A man may well lose himself in Richmond Park, as I know from tiresome experience. And beyond the Park . . . admittedly . . . lies London. But I have always felt that it is really a very long way off, in a completely different world, that it lacks all substance. If you stand on one of the little hills of the Park you can see London in the distance, but it looks as though it were the backcloth to a child's theatre, all tinsel and cardboard, and you can cock a snook at it. You need not be frightened by it—as sane men must be frightened by all cities. (Anybody who can look at the Empire State Building without a feeling of alarm and despair must be, *ipso facto*, nuts.) Here in the Park you are safe, with your feet on the sweet, soft turf, and the wild deer grazing, and the venerable oaks lifting their arms in perpetual prayer to an untainted sky.

That is our background. And if this were a different kind of opus I could meander about in it for ever. But as this is a scientific work, written with an eye to the veterinary surgeon book-reading public—which I gather is enormous, and largely untapped—we must reluctantly leave the Park, and wander home through the silver birch woods to Ham Common.

Which brings us to the next section

COTTAGE

When we have done with this section, the scene will be finally set.

One of the nicest things that ever happened to me was when the President of the Royal Academy suddenly arrived at the cottage on a hot Sunday afternoon, stumped out into the middle of the lawn, demanded a paper and pencil, and began to draw. And then, when he had made a number of enchanting sketches of eaves and windows and porticoes, turned to me with a little smile and said:

'This is a Jane Austen house; this is a *tender* house.'

No doubt many members of the Virile School of Modern Prose, wielding their pens with a force that might be more suitably employed for the harpooning of whales, would resent the suggestion that they lived in a 'tender' house. To me, the adjective is apposite and consoling, particularly when I recall the distinction of the man who made it—a man who is among the most considerable architects of our age.

How can we convey this 'tenderness'? Perhaps we might begin at the front door. This looks out on to a pocket-handkerchief of a garden—the main garden, of course, is at the back—which I have deliberately kept as 'cottagey' as possible. The white latticed porch (*circa* 1800) could hardly be prettier. It screamed for a honeysuckle and got it, and if I knew a very old lady, permanently wrapped in shawls, with a penchant for sitting in porches, I should hire her by the hour. Just by the porch there is the aforesaid lemon-verbena, for crunching and sniffing purposes on one's exits and entrances. (It is heart-rending to think that there must be quite large numbers of people who have to go to work every morning without

the soothing anodyne of a pinch of lemon-verbena; one cannot imagine how they get through the day.) The path up to the porch is lined, needless to say, with lavender. There is a raised bed in the centre for wallflowers in the spring and pinks in the summer, which cluster round the feet of a little eighteenth-century statue in lead—a boy playing a flute. I am always afraid that one day somebody will come and steal him, but I have put such appalling curses on anybody who might do so, and woven such hideous spells against any possible marauder, that the atmosphere round the figure is probably charged with sufficient menace to act as a deterrent.

Add a shrub of rosemary in one corner, a clump of madonna lilies in another, a row of floribunda roses under the white railings, and you have the front garden.

Let us step inside.

Ahead of us is a narrow staircase, with a simple but elegant balustrade of pitch pine. We can now remind ourselves that this is supposed to be a book about cats, for it is fairly certain that 'Five' will be reposing on the sixth step. (He chooses the sixth step because there is a hot water pipe concealed in the wall behind it.) He lies at full length, with his tail dangling down, and since the step is narrow and 'Five' is inclined to be plump, he slightly bulges over the edge. He is something of an obstacle to traffic between the two floors, but he is never disturbed. Or almost never. We

once had a very disagreeable daily woman who was afflicted—probably rightly—by rheumatism, and one day she was discovered pushing 'Five' out of the way with her foot. It need hardly be said that her reign came to an abrupt conclusion and for a short time the spells and curses which were normally used for the protection of the little boy in the front garden were transferred, with increased vehemence, in her direction.

We open a door on the left and—minding the step—we enter the principal room in the house. This, of course, is the music room. Where the piano is, there is one's treasure, as far as I am concerned. It is a long, low room which was formerly two, looking out on to the lawn. Today it is white and sunny and sparkling, but when I first saw it my heart sank; it was so dark that even on the brightest of mornings one would have to turn on the electric light before one could play the piano. This would be intolerable, for nothing, surely, is more delightful than sitting down at the piano on a summer day, and playing Chopin or Debussy while the natural sunlight drifts over one's shoulders through the vines outside, creating a filigree of shadow on the printed page . . . a shifting pattern of ghostly leaf and blossom that dances to the mood of the music.

The main cause of this darkness came from a giant copper beech whose sombre arms stretched right over the roof, and I had not been in residence for a couple of days before my heart was sinking lower than ever, for two reasons.

Firstly, because I knew that the copper beech would have to come down and because it is hateful to destroy a beautiful tree.

Secondly, because the cottage was Crown property, and because the lease contained a clause that no tree could be cut down without the permission of the Crown Commissioners.

Having a somewhat vivid imagination I immediately transformed the Commissioners, in my mind's eye, into evil implacable monsters with horns, whose sole purpose in life was to condemn me to perpetual darkness. It never occurred to me, for one moment, that they might in fact be normal human beings, amenable to reason. When Gaskin suggested that I should write to them and explain the situation I could hardly believe my ears. How could he make such an astonishing proposal? How *could* one write to such creatures? Where did they live? . . . What did they look like? Did Gaskin know? Of course not. Nobody knew anything about the

Crown Commissioners. All one knew, with certainty, was that they had horns, that they spent their lives plotting misery for people like myself. And that they were not in the telephone book.

So months were wasted trying to devise means by which we could rid ourselves of the copper beech without the knowledge, let alone the assistance, of the hated Crown Commissioners. We tried the most powerful spells and incantation, without effect. We got up in the small hours of the morning and crawled along the wall, and nipped off small branches here and there, but the more we nipped the more gigantic the tree seemed to become. To tackle the problem in this manner would take years and obviously, before we had finished it, the horned ones would be upon us. One night, in a local pub, I talked loudly and despairingly of my affliction, in the mood of Henry II when he cried for the death of Thomas Becket. 'Who will rid me of this pestilent beech?' I demanded. On the following morning I was called upon by an exceptionally sinister youth of seafaring origin, who had overheard the conversation. He had a touch of the tarbrush, and 'I love Mum' tattooed across the knuckles of his left hand, which is always a bad sign. He told me that he was an expert in poisoning trees, and as he was quite obviously an expert in poisoning practically anything, I showed him the door. A moment later, in a state of nervous prostration, I was ringing up the Crown Commissioners. They *were* in the telephone book, after all.

A few days later 'they' came down, in the shape of a nice young man in a bowler hat, which, when removed, betrayed no trace of horns. He refused the outsize dry martinis which I offered him in order that he might be stunned into a mood of acquiescence. He paced round the copper beech, he went in and out of the house, he examined the walls, went into the house again, talked to Gaskin, came back. For a moment I had a terrible feeling that he might have horns after all. Then he delivered his decision. Of course the copper beech must come down. It was not only darkening the house and impoverishing the garden, it was getting into the drains.

So down it came, one bright July morning, with a thud that shook the earth like a giant fist and set all the dogs barking for miles around. And I had all the usual feelings of remorse and self-reproach when I saw the proud branches humbled and withering. But the cottage breathed a sigh of relief; it was almost as though you could see the lattice windows blinking and opening their eyes to the light that had so long been denied them.

This book is getting out of hand. There are cats to the right of us, cats to the left of us, purring, mewing, scratching in the wings, but I cannot seem to get them on the stage. All because I am taking so long in hanging the backcloth.

But please bear with me for a few more pages. Cats make such exquisite entrances that they deserve a proper setting. If a Siamese cat were to appear at the top of the staircase in the Savoy Hotel, and slowly, haughtily descend to the main dining-room, tail erect, all the women would be put to shame. The dowagers would retreat to the Ladies' and then go home. The more intelligent of the models, it is hoped, would take out their pencils, and make notes.

So we must go back to the music room, into which the light is now flooding, after the decease of the copper beech, flooding and streaming in aqueous ripples of light that flicker round the fireplace and over the keys of the piano.

But the room was still not light enough. Cottage rooms, however picturesque, very seldom are. So I devised a plan which, in its turn, led to a story. And when I have told it, the cats at last can take the stage. We will call it . . .

THE STORY OF THE THREE MIRRORS

It happened like this. My plan for the music room was very simple —to cover the darkest wall with squares of old mirror which would echo the sunlight and bring the sparkle of life to a moribund corner. In case you think that mirrored walls are reminiscent of bathrooms in smart hotels, I can assure you that this was not the idea at all. The effect I wanted was more like a tapestry of faded silver. All the pieces of glass would have to be old and softened by the fingers of time, and they would have to blend into the wall as though they had hung there for ever.

So I sent for Mr Barnes, the local builder, otherwise known as Hamlet. We have called him Hamlet because whenever a job is suggested to him he sighs deeply, folds his arms, and steps aside, wrapped in melancholy, and stares at whatever has to be done, soliloquizing. I can never quite catch what he is saying; it is probably only something to do with paint and plaster; but the sighs are so profound, and his features are so sicklied o'er with the pale cast of thought, that the effect is most moving. When I told him about the mirror idea, he was literally shaken with sighs, and he began to murmur with more than usual emotion. In the end, however, it transpired that he was only making notes about the nature of the frame that would be needed to support the pieces of glass. He suggested that I should advertise for old mirrors in the *Richmond and Twickenham Times*.

Which I did. And in due course I received a number of replies, most of them unhelpful and one of them, to put it mildly, bizarre. It might be thought that an advertisement for old-fashioned mirrors would be the last thing to evoke any suggestion of impropriety, but this was obviously the effect that it had on a certain elderly gentleman living on the outskirts of Twickenham. From his letter I gathered that as a young man in the Navy he had spent a number of riotous nights in a certain glittering establishment in Marseilles, where the ladies could be watched from behind specially treated transparent mirrors, without realizing that they were being observed. One of these mirrors he had annexed, and he offered to sell it to me. I am not a great expert on these matters, and though I have often heard of trick mirrors I have never been quite clear about who watches whom or who sees what . . . let alone why anybody bothers to do either. So I did not answer the letter. But I could not help thinking that it must be rather mournful, after a youth of such sauciness, to end one's days as an old gentleman on the outskirts of Twickenham, with nothing to look at but one's own face.

That is the curious story of the first mirror. An equally curious episode is recalled by the second. It came from a little pub in Hampton—one of those modest inns where you feel the customers are all members of a big family. I called out of business hours and was greeted at the side door by an immensely fat lady with marigold hair, cerise lips, and so much costume jewellery that she could have furnished a Christmas tree without missing anything.

The woman gave me a jolly smile, said 'pleased to meet you', and led me through the empty bar to a large shed at the back, that was filled with a clutter of junk. There, leaning against the wooden wall, was a large mirror, six foot by six, just what I wanted, with a nice dim patina.

She asked only three pounds for it, which I paid her on the spot. When the bargain was completed, she turned and looked back at her reflection —a grotesque, monstrous, unnaturally swollen reflection—hung with all those baubles.

'In a way I'll be sorry to let it go.' There was a catch in her voice. 'When I was training for the ballet I used to do my exercises in front of that old mirror. Dreamed of doing *Swan Lake*, I did.' She forced a smile, and threw up her head, trying for a moment to defeat her double chins. Then she sagged back to normal. 'Some Swan!' She gave me a rather sad little wink, and led the way out.

The last mirror was leaning against a wall in the parlour of a small shabby house that stood on a backwater of the Thames. You could see the river running in it, deep and silent, like a green ribbon fluttering over the silver surface. If you had been standing by my side you would also have seen its owner—a little woman in black, who spoke in a low, sweet voice. Years ago, she must have been as pretty as they come, and even now her cheeks had the clear pink of wild roses—a pink that flushed gently as she spoke:

'I am afraid it is not in very good condition,' she was saying. 'You can see for yourself; the frame is badly chipped, and there is a crack right across the centre.'

'I shan't be using the frame. And it doesn't matter about the crack, because I shall be cutting it up.'

'Cutting it up?' She glanced at me, and for a moment I thought she was going to make some protest. Then she looked back in the mirror and nodded to herself. 'I see.'

'I hope you won't mind that.'

'It will hardly be my concern when I have sold it.' She went on staring into the mirror. 'It is just that it has sentimental associations.'

Suddenly I realized that she was acutely lonely, and that she was longing to talk to somebody . . . anybody . . . before the mirror went out of her life.

Then she told me the story—the simplest and most hackneyed of stories, but for some reason it moved me deeply. It happened nearly fifty years ago, at the beginning of the First World War, when the shabby little house had not been so shabby, when the garden had not been rank and overgrown, and when trim lawns had stretched down to the river, lawns on which there were elegant tea-parties, and young men who had danced attendance—young men who, as the summer faded, changed from their white flannels into the khaki that was to become the sombre habit of a doomed generation. Among these young men was one in particular who fell in love with her, and she with him. He came to say goodbye on March 15, 1915. Why I recall that date I do not know—perhaps because the old lady remembered it herself so intensely. He went out by the front door, and she came back to the parlour, to be by herself, to think, to try to be brave. Then she heard a tap on the window. She looked up and there he was reflected in the mirror, smiling and waving; he had walked round the house for a last glimpse of her.

'He walked backwards, over the lawn, waving and smiling. I waved too, but I was crying, and I did not want him to see, so I turned away again, and watched him in the mirror.' Her voice was quite calm . . . there was even the shadow of a smile on her own face. 'I remember that the crocuses were out, and I was afraid that he would step on them. But he noticed them, just in time.'

She never saw him again. He was killed a week later.

At length the two mirrors were delivered, together with a number of other strips and pieces, all of which had their own stories which there is no space to tell. And when I sit at the piano, and play the music that I love, by sunlight, by candlelight, in the dusk of an April evening, the silvered wall that faces me seems like the backcloth of a tiny theatre that is peopled by ghosts . . . the ghosts of the wicked ladies of Marseilles, the ghost of a young dancer, laughing and flicking her fingers, and the ghost of a girl standing at a window, waving, with tears in her eyes, tears which misted the gold of the crocuses. 'I was afraid that he would step on them.'

So now at last the scene is set—enough of it for our purpose. And to assure you that this indeed is going to be a book about cats, I may mention that all the cats, in their various ways, were deeply interested in the mirrored wall as soon as it was completed. Oscar was inclined to be skittish with it, and dabbed at himself. 'Five', who has Narcissus tendencies, sat in front of it and stared into his own green eyes for such long periods that when he eventually tore himself away he looked quite dopey. It was left to 'Four' to pretend that the mirrors were hostile and full of baneful influences. And so, although he is an elderly and quite sophisticated cat who knows all about mirrors, he would stroll innocently past the wall and then—always provided that he had an audience—register sudden terror, and slink away, glancing backwards as though Coleridge's fearful fiend were treading close behind him.

DRAWERS

Let us hasten to explain that this chapter is in no way concerned with ladies' and gentlemen's underwear. The drawers to which we refer belong to bureaux, tallboys, and such-like. As soon as we have opened them, pussy, by some mysterious instinct, is aware of what we are up to, and appears from nowhere, in order to leap into the drawers, inspect their contents, and if necessary curl up and go to sleep on them.

I have a few decent pieces of furniture. One of them is a walnut tallboy which I bought from an old gentleman called Mr Crowther who lived in an astonishing blend of splendour and confusion at Syon Lodge, surrounded by acres of exquisite temples, urns, cherubs, fountains, and Regency commodes, which he sold at erratic prices to the nobility and gentry . . . and occasionally to people such as myself. (I say 'erratic' because if he liked you he took ten per cent off the bill and if he didn't he put ten per cent on.)

Back to the tallboy. Forty pounds it was, and it should have been eighty. There it stands in my bedroom, slim and elegant, and you would not think that it had any psychic qualities. But it must have some power of communication, for as soon as I open one of its drawers, particularly if it is a drawer containing some newly laundered dress shirts, Oscar appears from nowhere, and either leaps into it unasked or—if it is too high— demands in no uncertain terms that he should be lifted up and put inside.

Fs will agree that these demands should be granted, though on wet days, when pussy has just come in from the garden, it is first permissible to sponge the paws and wipe them dry. For some reason which I have never been able to fathom, the drawer containing the dress shirts is always the favourite, although it is at the top and shallower than the rest of them, and although the shirts are covered in cold, crackly Cellophane. One would have thought that the bottom drawer, which is much more commodious and is comfortably lined with socks and woollen pullovers, would have been more popular. But no—the top drawer it must be, and there Oscar sits, purring and crackling, with his large, square, whiskered face protruding over the edge. If I slightly close the drawer, which he seems to like, he looks like some strange Cheshire cat in one of Alice's unrecorded adventures.

I have often wondered if this almost universal feline desire to curl up in drawers is an example of the Return-to-the-Womb complex—which, once one has recovered from the initial shock of the idea, seems to make very good sense. Put very simply it implies a compulsion to escape from the turmoil of the world with its strident noises and its harsh lights, and to go back into the dark, quiet mystery from which we came. This desire has sometimes been compared with the Death Wish, but the analogy, I think, is false. It is not a wish for death, but for innocence, and rebirth, and above all, for peace.

True or false, the Return-to-the-Womb complex is probably present, in varying degrees, in all of us. Carried to its logical conclusion it leads to lunacy. During the last tragic months of his life Nijinsky spent day after day curled up on his bed in the shape of a foetus, with the cold Swiss sunlight shining down on an ageing body—the same body that had once enraptured the world as it danced to the silver flutes of Debussy's faun.

But this shadow should not have fallen across our page. I think that it can be sent scurrying with a smile, and a story. When a certain darling of the intelligentsia first had the complex explained to him he nodded, and flicked the ash from his cigarette. And then he said: 'I am sure that all this is true because I have the same desire myself. But . . . it *must* be a Womb with a View.'

EDUCATION

To say that cats cannot be educated would be untrue; they are creatures of high intelligence and sensibility whose native reactions can be trained and directed. But they certainly cannot be drilled or regimented.

Dogs—yes. One can well imagine a platoon of poodles marching stiffly up and down the barrack square, and liking it. One can see them wheeling and doubling, sloping arms and presenting tails, in strict obedience to the hoarse barks of their sergeant-major. Cats, never.

(Now one comes to think of it, is it not significant that sergeant-majors of fiction invariably *bark?* They never mew. A sergeant-major who mewed—though personally I should dote on such a phenomenon—would seldom be recommended for a commission.)

This intransigence, this refusal to 'come to heel', in any sense of that unpleasantly despotic phrase, is one of the reasons why the true F finds such delight in feline companionship. He is aware that if a cat seeks him out it does so of its own free will, not because it is obeying a shouted command or pricking up its ears at a blow on the whistle. All the same, in the interests of domestic harmony, there are times when a little gentle discipline may be desirable. Hence our invention of the dinner gong.

We do not, of course, use a real gong, we merely tap a plate for the evening meal. There is no need to do this at breakfast time; every morning at seven o'clock there is a great waving of tails, lifting of paws, a brisk mewing and purring under the kitchen sink. But at tea-time it is different; the cats may be asleep, or working in the garden, or engaged on tours of inspection, or some form of espionage. So we use the 'gong' to summon them.

This is the drill. At half past four, precisely, Gaskin lays down his copy of the evening paper, emerges from his sitting-room, and goes into the tool-shed, where a saucepan containing three whiting is reposing on top of an old gas stove. (This may sound obscure. What is an old gas stove doing in the tool-shed? Your guess is as good as mine. All I know is that it is there, and that it is quite safe, because there is no gas in it.)

Then the whiting are put on three plates and carried to their appointed positions ... Oscar's in a corner under the sink, 'Four's' by the refrigerator, and 'Five's' on the kitchen table. (Under 'Heat' I explain the deep psychological reasons which have impelled 'Five' to dine in this elevated position.)

All is now set. Gaskin takes another plate and taps it sharply and expertly—*con brio* would be the musical direction—with a fork.

Whereupon, several things happen. The first is a resounding 'plonk' from upstairs, as Oscar leaps off my bed. (Oscar is always the first to 'enter the dining-room', which is only natural, because he is the largest, the youngest, and the most energetic.) The plonk is followed by a tumble of paws down the stairs. A moment later, Oscar is dining. Next, there will be the gentle rattle of the cat-door, which signifies the entrance of 'Four'. He has almost certainly come from his watch-tower on the top of the tool-shed. As the eldest and most responsible of the cats, he selected this post from the first day of our arrival in the cottage. From here he has a wide view over all the neighbouring territory. He can keep a constant vigil on any suspicious movements by Rudolf and Webster—the cats next door. He can also keep an eye on the gardener, warn the birds off the crocuses under the copper beech, and, when autumn comes, restrain the activities of the grey squirrels who come for the nuts on the old walnut tree. If it were not for 'Four', sitting in his watch-tower, lashing his tail, I should never have a walnut at all.

The last to answer the summons of the gong is 'Five'. Although he is the plumpest, he seems to have the smallest appetite. He walks in slowly and rather haughtily, like an elderly gentleman in an expensive residential hotel making his way to his favourite corner. One feels that there should be a copy of *The Times* under his arm, and half a bottle of Médoc waiting for him, and a tin of Bath Oliver biscuits. Even when he jumps on the table he retains a certain 'hauteur'. Unlike Oscar he does not tuck in immediately; he yawns, glances round the room, sniffs, and then gives the whiting a languid dab before beginning, very daintily, to dispose of it.

This section seems to have been devoted more to Eating than to Education, but we hope that the reader will not take this amiss, in view of the fact that most of us learn the first elements of civilized behaviour at the dinner table.

As it is with eating, so it is with all the other aspects of feline educa-tion. We do not command cats, we coax them; we do not issue orders to them, we make suggestions. Sometimes, we even appeal to their sense of pity, as in the case of Oscar and the chairs. The only really effective way of stopping Oscar from ripping the upholstery is to emit a wail of anguish as soon as he begins, as though one's very flesh were being rent. And since Oscar has a fondness for one, and is quick to interpret human moods, he nearly always desists, and walks across, with a look of deep concern on his face, and rubs against one's legs to express his contrition.

But by and large, the cats remain untamed—wild creatures in a

domestic setting, lions of the hearthrug, at nobody's beck and call. And this, surely, is in accordance with the conception of nature. For though man likes to think of himself as a lord of creation, this is a title which he can never earn. He may picture himself as towering above the humbler inhabitants of the universe, with undisputed dominion over fur and feather and fin, but in reality he has not the smallest dominion over any living creature. There is only one way in which he can prove his 'superiority', and that is by inflicting the death sentence. He cannot even alter the course of an ant, except by stamping on it.

To me, this is consoling. Man, in his relations with the animals, is only too apt to get above himself—to 'get on his high horse' in more senses than one. It is good that he should occasionally be reminded of his impotence, in all except this matter of inflicting the death sentence. He can shoot a pheasant, but not by a hair's breadth can he deflect the lovely design that is traced by a seagull's wings as it sweeps between the sky and the drifting spray. He can harpoon a whale; he can employ all the devices of the internal combustion engine as he flashes past in his speed-boat, tugging at some creature that he has dragged from the depths. But he cannot call the humblest minnow to his command.

And never—but never—can he control a cat.

FLOWERS

Cats and flowers have played so large a part in my life that I can scarcely think of one without the other. In a cluster of wild hyacinths I can see reflected the blue eyes of my first Siamese; on warm May mornings he would wander to the shadow of an old wall where the hyacinths had come by chance, and dispose himself most elegantly upon them. If reproached for squashing the hyacinths, he merely blinked; the blue eyes and the blue flowers, mingling together, were so beautiful that there was nothing to be done about it.

Let us take a walk in the garden, to pick a bunch of flowers and bring it indoors and arrange it on a table by the piano, observing, meanwhile, how greatly we are assisted in our task by 'Four', 'Five', and Oscar.

But first, that word 'arrange' has started a train of thought which reminds me that there is something I must get off my chest, though it has no direct connection with cats. It concerns the art of flower-decoration.

This has become such a racket that nowadays if one were to do anything so simple as to pick a bunch of daffodils and drop them at random into a jam jar—which is probably how van Gogh would have chosen to paint them—one would be regarded as a Philistine. Or if, like Fantin-Latour, one disposed a few sprays of white roses in a silver bowl, and let them take their hazard of casual beauty against the breeze of an open window, one would be called to account for not sticking them in a pin-holder. Today, one must create 'significant form'. (I wonder if the women who natter about flower arrangements ever studied the works of Roger

Fry?) One must have a 'musical line' or some such nonsense, and the eye must be 'brought to a central point', and the 'colour masses' must be properly balanced, etc etc.

I am criticizing, of course, the professional flower decorators, those well-meaning ladies who are for ever writing and lecturing and rushing all over the place telling their defenceless sisters what to do and how to do it. There are thousands of women who—left to their own devices—produce exquisite arrangements without ever having heard of 'vertical lines' balanced by 'harmonious triangles' or any such balderdash. My mother was one of them. She could take a spray of bramble and a few brown kitchen-garden chrysanthemums and set them in a pewter mug, and the result was magical.

But the professionals! There are a few blessed exceptions, but one wishes that most of them would go and do it at the greengrocer's, and leave the flowers alone. Consider the tortures to which they subject that poor little bunch of daffodils. Firstly, in a desperate attempt to be 'original' —how dare anybody be 'original' with a daffodil?—they group their horrid messes round a china figure. Probably a nasty little lamb from Copenhagen with a catkin stuck into its behind. Then they proceed to chop off the stalks of the daffodils, to varying lengths, to get their precious 'significant form'. Finally—this is the crowning blasphemy—they so dispose the daffodils that half of them are lying in a horizontal position, as though they had been battered by a violent rain-storm.

After which they transport their 'creations' to the local flower show where doubtless they will be awarded a prize by one of their buddies.

I must check this outburst, but it had to come. I have always thought that there is only one sin—cruelty. These women are guilty of cruelty to flowers.

We may now return, faintly flushed, to the garden—and the cats. This is the drill.

I am half way down the herbaceous border, with the first flowers gathered into the trug basket over my arm. When I began picking, at the far end, under the copper beech, the idea was to make a white bunch, which explains the cluster of white campanulas and the creamy sprays of deutzia. But then, as I stepped into the sunlight, there was a tendril of pale

yellow clematis on the wall, which would look very pretty trailing over the edge of the vase. (If only one could get it to trail the right way round! Clematis is a maddening flower to arrange; it always seems to want to stand on its head.) So now the whole plan is changed. It must be a white and yellow bunch; we must go and look for some more yellows.

So here we are deep in thought, making lovely designs and colour schemes, and in all probability behaving as tiresomely as the aforesaid despised lady-decorators.

And then there is a faint tug at the basket. I look round, like a fisherman surprised by a bite. I observe that a piece of bass is trailing from the basket on to the lawn, and at the end of the bass, pouncing, is 'Five'.

At this point a faint sigh is permitted. For 'Five's' gesture cannot go unrewarded; the basket must be put down, the bass must be twitched and jerked and wiggled about, and one must run across the lawn trailing the bass, at least once, with 'Five' in hot pursuit. But all this is fatiguing and one wants to get on with the flowers and one wishes that 'Five' had chosen another time for dalliance.

However, there is an effective way of dealing with these situations, which I will pass on to fellow Fs. Two years ago, in a similar dilemma, I happened to remember that 'Five' liked sitting in baskets, particularly if they were far too small for him. So I removed the flowers, and put them in a bucket under the copper beech. Then, returning to 'Five', I pushed him over on his back, scooped him up, and inserted him sideways into the trug basket, pushing him down under the handle and moulding him in, as though one were kneading a loaf. These attentions, to my relief, were well received, and when I lifted up the basket, he stayed in it quite placidly, purring, with his tail hanging over the edge. We were both pleased with ourselves; 'Five' was diverted by this new method of transport, which gave him an opportunity of seeing the lupins at eye-level; and I had all the agreeable sensations of taking baby out in the pram.

So now, when I go out to gather a mixed bunch, there are always two baskets. One for the flowers and one for 'Five'.

I am sure that cats love flowers, or at least, that there is some sort of mystic attraction between them. It cannot be by pure chance that a Siamese always seeks out blue flowers, to go with his eyes. We have already met my beloved 'One', a king among cats, as he lay by the wild hyacinths. But he also chose to dispose himself among clumps of delphiniums and love-in-the-mist. Always blue.

The primary attraction, presumably, is one of scent. Here cats are more drawn to the kitchen-garden. They seem to be unmoved by the perfume of roses or magnolias or such-like, but they do a great deal of very pretty and intense sniffing round a bed of lovage or tarragon or apple mint. And, of course, valerian.

The mention of valerian brings me in reluctant opposition to that formidable old gentleman Mr W. Robinson. In his classic volume *The English Flower Garden*, he is contemptuous of this amiable and nostalgic plant. I call it 'amiable' because it will grow in a handful of dust on a windswept wall. And 'nostalgic' because it brings to mind many summer hours of childhood, when it brushed my cheeks as I climbed the cliffs of Land's End, to the challenge of the smooth, dark seas below, and the cry of the seagulls all around.

Mr Robinson considers that the valerian is a 'common' plant and he proclaims, on page 678 of the sixteenth edition of his otherwise admirable book, that the flowers are 'unpleasantly scented'. This statement lays Mr Robinson open to grave suspicions of being non-F. For how could a flower be 'common' or 'unpleasantly scented' when its odour, throughout the summer months, attracts a long train of royal—if somewhat scruffy—personages, who stalk proudly up to it, sniff it, and then, turning their backs . . . But let this picture dissolve, as it were, in a cloud of perfumed prose.

And let us ring down the curtain on a quiet garden, during a sultry afternoon in July, with the cats disposed in their accustomed positions. Oscar, stretched out among the rushes by the pond, occasionally extending a languid paw over the water, as a fish darts by with a flash of silver. 'Four', a limp, languid lump of fur, curled up on the parched earth in the shadow of the old white rose tree, that occasionally lets a snowy petal flutter down on to his back, so that he twitches and opens a green eye, and then goes to sleep again.

And 'Five', gravely stalking me as I go out to pick the flowers, with the bass trailing behind. And being lifted up, and moulded into the spare basket, and being carried round in a stately promenade.

So now you will realize why, when I look into a bunch of flowers, I always seem to see the gleam of cats' eyes through the blossom.

GRAVES AND EPITAPHS

A gloomy subject? That depends on your view of life—and of death.

One of the happiest and most tranquil places I ever visited was the animals' sanctuary in Tangier. I had motored out there in a truck belonging to the People's Dispensary for Sick Animals. I was in need of solace. The Arabs are not renowned for their kindness to animals;[1] they are not deliberately cruel, but they seem incapable of realizing that animals can suffer at all or—even if they do realize it—that it is any concern of theirs. This was why I was thankful to escape for a while from the dark, winding alleys of Tangier, where skeletal dogs slunk shivering into the darkness, and starving cats fought for scraps of dusty skin and bone under the barrows in the fish market.

The sanctuary was five miles from the city, on the way to the bare, saffron-coloured hills. It lay off the main road in a gentle curving valley, through which there ran a stream on whose banks a group of women were drying the weekly wash. It was a cool, clear day of brilliant sunshine; there was a hint of spring in the air; the fields were starred with white

[1] Thanks to the P.D.S.A. there has been a marked improvement since my visit.

narcissi and under the bare trees there were pools of white violets. I remember thinking how gay and pleasant a picture it all made—the white sheets the women were washing, the white flowers in the meadows, all under the cold, clean, blue sky.

We turned off the rutted track and took the path to the cemetery, neatly disposed in a near-by field, with wild almonds blooming around. About a hundred animals were buried there, mostly cats and dogs that had been brought over from England to end their days by the side of their masters and mistresses. A few of the graves were overgrown, but most of them were tidy and well-tended, and on several there were fresh flowers, violets, and narcissi from the local fields, sprays of mimosa from the hedgerows on the hill. Each grave had a name engraved on it, and often there were simple mottoes and tags of verse which I will not quote; out of their context they might sound foolish.

But that was not how they seemed to me, standing there under the young almond trees with nothing but the tinkling of the stream to break the silence. Inevitably—and doubtless with blatant sentimentality—I recalled Rupert Brooke. 'If I should die, think only this of me: That there's some corner of a foreign field That is for ever England. There shall be In that rich earth a richer dust concealed . . .'

No, a very humble dust, mingling with the alien soil of Africa. This dust was all that was left of many greatly loved little creatures, dogs who had snuffled through the bracken of English moors, cats who had scampered over the lawns of English gardens—little creatures who had given many hours of delight and laughter to their masters and mistresses —and in their passing, had left a great sadness. Was it so foolish, so sentimental, that the delight should be honoured and the grief commemorated?

Maybe I am the wrong person to write these words. Concerning the disposition of my own remains, 'I couldn't care less'—a vulgar phrase, but apposite. If one believes in the survival of the spirit, what happens to the body is surely of the smallest importance? They can do anything they like with my own. As long as—to quote the immortal remark of Mrs Patrick Campbell, when she was discussing certain forms of illicit love-making—'as long as they don't do it in the street and frighten the horses'.

But somehow, with animals it is different. Perhaps this is because they were cast in such humble roles while they were alive that when they are dead we feel the need of making a belated gesture to acknowledge their importance. For after all, the very fact that they *have* died makes them important; they are a step further on the road; they have seen through the curtain, even if the eyes are those of a dead kitten, lying in the gutter. They have achieved this importance, as Thomas Hardy wrote, 'by crossing at a breath, into safe and shielded death'. And merely because they have 'taken hence their insignificance' they

> Loom as largened to the sense,
> Shape as part, above man's will,
> Of the Imperturbable.

This same thought moved an American poet when she wrote:

> What was warm is strangely cold—
> When dissolved the little breath?
> How could this small body hold
> So immense a thing as Death?[1]

That is why a grave for an animal is neither ridiculous nor illogical, and why this little sanctuary at Tangier was one of the most moving places I have ever visited.

When we left I strolled up into the hills to pick mimosa—an activity which has a special thrill of its own. To be able to gather up armfuls of this golden blossom, without paying for it, gives one something of the sensation of robbing a bank. Then I sat down and looked back over the valley towards the sanctuary and thought how nice it would be to be buried in it oneself. Perhaps one could reserve a small plot? I had noticed a blank space under one of the almond trees, between two Scotch pussies, who had lived to a great age, and a Devonshire bulldog. They would be pleasant companions in the Elysian fields. Yes, it would be a very nice place indeed, but I doubted whether it could be arranged. Somebody would be sure to object; and it is quite possible there would be something against it in the Prayer Book. Besides, I did not really crave even so meek a sepulchre—not for myself.

[1] 'For a Dead Kitten'—Sara Hay

But for 'Four' and 'Five' and Oscar it would be different. Indeed, as I sat on the hillside staring across the valley, with the golden blossoming treasure resting on my knees, I found myself devising the most superior mausoleums to suit their various personalities. 'Four's' would be of jet, with a frieze of golden claws. 'Five's' would be faintly feminine and decidedly rococo, and the walls would be encrusted with festoons of peridots. Oscar's would be very striking, with a vaulted ceiling decorated by the fins of fishes, executed in jade.

A plague on these premature forebodings! At the moment of writing, all the cats are so brimful of health and spirits that I strongly suspect—and hope—that they will be the principal participants in my own cortège. That will indeed give them a glorious opportunity to exhibit their special talents. 'Four', the Cat Who Does the Act, will never have had a more moving role. I can see him, as I have often seen him, jet black, head sunk in grief, tail trailing to the mournful lilt of Chopin's funeral march. (One hopes that he will have some sort of audience, apart from Gaskin and the daily woman.) Oscar, I know, will bear himself like a man, though I hope that he does not make any of his heartbreaking little snuffling noises, which he makes when he is sad, because I should be unable to get out of the coffin and comfort him.

And 'Five'? He will be at the back, paws moving strictly in rhythm, tail erect, whiskers shining. But his ears will be at the alert. For this would be an occasion where 'The Iceman Cometh'. Icemen, presumably, have much in common with dustmen. And we all know what 'Five' thinks about *them*.

HEAT

Once, during the war, in the depths of a bitter winter, I journeyed north to stay with Sir Compton Mackenzie on his island in the Hebrides, for some obscure reason which I am sure that both of us have forgotten.

And there, sitting on top of a hot stove in the kitchen, were four elderly Siamese cats.

It was a most impressive moment in one's life.

Outside, the winds howled and raged through the stunted pines. Icy spray lashed the windows and the paths were strewn with tattered sea-weed. The witches of *Macbeth* would have been in their element, and the whole occasion was made the more melodramatic by the fact that the whole island was alive with illicit lights. The inhabitants, with a fine Scottish independence and a lofty disregard for 'enemy action'—how dated that nasty phrase sounds today!—paid small heed to the black-out which was smothering the South. With the result that through the scream of the wind and the hiss of the rain I fancied that I heard the menacing growl of hostile aircraft.

Against this lurid background the elderly Siamese cats sat on the burning stove, gazing with veiled blue eyes into the distance, thinking lofty Siamese thoughts. They reminded me of four Eastern ladies of the utmost distinction giving their fatigued attention to some ceremonial occasion. The only thing that worried me about this touching episode was that their sit-upons might be scorched.

I approached the stove, held out my arms to the eldest and most imperial of the cats, and, after making the proper obeisances, was successful in persuading it to be gently elevated. (This round-about phrase may perhaps only be understood by advanced Fs. A non-F would write 'I picked it up.' I did no such thing. I repeat—'I was successful in persuading it to be gently elevated.' If this distinction is not crystal clear, you must put down this work and take the corgi for a walk.)

And I discovered that the Siamese's sit-upon was, indeed, scorching. I will not go so far as to say that I could not bear my hand on it, but if one's own sit-upon had been half as hot one would have been in great distress. Yet, here was this sensitive creature, quite unmoved. Mentally baptizing her Honourable Lady Hot-Situpon of the Northern Isles I rearranged her on the top of the stove. You will not be surprised to learn that the moment her sit-upon touched the stove, she began to purr, like a kettle when you put it back on the gas ring.

The whole subject of cats and heat is absorbing, not only biologically but psychologically. The devices they employ in their efforts to keep warm shed a revealing light on their characters.

Consider 'Four'—the Cat Who Does the Act. He invariably takes advantage of any cold spell to put on a virtuoso exhibition of being maltreated. Although he has a comfortable armchair next to the radiator in Gaskin's room—or for that matter, a corner of several warm beds and plenty of room in the linen cupboard—he scorns such obvious resorts. They afford no scope for his talents.

So what happens? 'Four', heaving tragic sighs, and casting agonized looks over his shoulder, stalks heavily to the fire-place in the music room. And then—poor forsaken creature—he curls up beside the dying ash, and disposes himself to sleep. Time and again I have gone up to him and said ' "Four", you are being too ridiculous. The wood-ash will be cold by the morning. What is more, it will get on your tail, and when you lick it off, it will get into your system. And though wood-ash is very good for lupins I cannot believe that it is good for elderly black cats. Apart from that, when you creep out in the morning, you will leave a trail of wood-ash all over the carpet, which will not be popular with Gaskin.'

But 'Four' pays no heed. He is far too engrossed in his role. So I shake my head, and bid him good-night, hoping that there will be no late callers to observe him crouched by the embers. Sure enough, in the morning he is still there, forlorn and hunched up, with a large blob of wood-ash on the end of his nose, when all he need do to get warm is walk a few yards to a blazing fire in the next room. There are no limits to the sacrifices which 'Four' will make in the exercise of his art.

'Five's' behaviour is equally revealing. 'Five', in spite of his deceptive *embonpoint*, is a bundle of nerves, owing to the unfortunate episode in his youth when he leapt out of an upstairs window while fleeing from a Pekinese. 'Five' is always the first to sound the tocsin on Tuesday mornings, when the dustmen come, rushing into the house from the garden with wild eyes and a bristling tail, as though the devil were at his heels. His choice of sleeping quarters, too, is always governed by strategic considerations; he likes to repose himself where nobody can come upon him unawares. For this reason his favourite spot is on a shelf at the top of the staircase, where he can lie, as in a watch-tower, with one green eye half open, on the look-out for any suspicious characters such as the grocer's boy.

And so, when winter strikes, when there is ice on the pond and the lawn is as hard as rock, and when I wrap up every morning in order to offer moral support to the delicate little eucalyptus trees in the far corner —for this is the only form of comfort I can give them and I believe it works—'Five' hies himself to the dark recesses of the linen cupboard. He walks upstairs slowly and sedately, with tail erect, sits outside the door, and emits a faint mew, which means: 'This is linen-cupboard weather. Kindly

let me in.' So we open the door, and he leaps up, progressing from shelf to shelf, till he reaches the top, where he curls up on an old patchwork and indicates, by a yawn, that he is quite comfortable and that one may take one's leave. He is warm, he is at ease, best of all, he is safe; even the dustmen would never think of looking for him here.

And Oscar? By now, you are probably enough in Oscar's confidence to guess that he does not greatly care how he keeps warm as long as he is in company. He would rather lie on a luke-warm lap than stretch himself before the brightest fire in an empty room. The front door has only to open, on a snowy night, and he will jump up from the sybaritic heat of the radiator, and start his welcome of weaving and curling before one has time to take off one's overcoat. Of all the cats I have ever known, Oscar is the most constant in his demand for human companionship; he is the classic answer to all those foolish slanders about feline cupboard love which are current in more barbaric outposts of the non-F world.

Which will be enough about Heat. Graver problems await us, so let us leave our little trio in their chosen places — 'Four' exhibiting his histrionic skill against the wood-ash, 'Five', betraying his complexes in the linen cupboard, and Oscar, curled up on a corner of my desk, making playful dabs at my pen. Which, I hope, may serve as an excuse for any occasional crudities in the composition of this opus.

INSOMNIA

I

    Cats are the best cure for insomnia that has yet been invented. In every well-appointed clinic for nervous diseases there should be a large Feline Annex, stocked with quantities of plump and amiable pussies, ready to be scooped up by expert attendants, carried down well-warmed corridors, and gently deposited on the unquiet beds of the insomniacs. The rest would be silence. Or even better than silence—gentle sighs and quiet purrs.

    Specially privileged patients, or those in the more acute stages, might be permitted to sleep in the Annex itself, on large, soft couches where they would receive the combined soporific attentions of several pussies at the same time. I have often thought that this would be the acme of sensuous delight, to be wafted to repose in an enormous living bundle of sleepy, purring fur.

    Of my three cats the most potent, as a 'knocker-outer', is 'Four'. By 'knocker-outer' I mean something like the red tablets one's doctor prescribes when the green ones are not strong enough. I am not a drug addict, and a single green one, taken about once a month, is enough for the normal routine. Sometimes, however, there is a crisis, and a nervous danger signal. Then I go to the medicine cupboard and take out the little bottle with the red tablets. But in nine cases out of ten I put it back again unopened, because I have remembered 'Four'. Why resort to expensive drugs when one can employ, free of charge, the services of inexpensive felines?

So I tiptoe downstairs, usually at about one a.m., and open the door of Gaskin's sitting-room, which is the room where 'Four' and 'Five' sleep when the weather is not cold enough for 'Four' to do his act or for 'Five' to seek the linen-cupboard.

There is 'Four', a small, densely black bundle, in the red armchair under the photograph of Edith Evans in *Evensong*. There too is 'Five', in the blue armchair under the photograph of himself sitting on the balustrade in the garden of 'Merry Hall'. Both cats open their eyes, and blink in the sudden light. Both immediately grasp the situation. 'Five' sends a sidelong glance to 'Four', which means 'This is where you have to do your stuff'. 'Four' gives a prodigious yawn, to indicate that he is drenched in an aura of sleep, which he is prepared to share with me.

Whereupon he rises, arches his back, stretches out his front paws, yawns again, shakes himself, and observes: 'I am at your disposal. You may carry me upstairs.'

Which I do. Even as he snuggles in my arms, negotiating the dark staircase, I have a feeling of relaxation. When I push open the door of my bedroom with my elbow the room seems strangely hushed. A few minutes ago the sounds drifting through the open window had been restless and disturbing; there had been an uneasy creak in the branches of the walnut tree and a tiresome rattle from the window blind. The screech owls had been unpleasantly close. But now the owls have flown away, and the wind has dropped, and the walnut tree has ceased its mutterings and is sighing itself to rest.

And so is 'Four'. As I deposit him on the bed, in the same scooped-up position, intact, he has forgotten all his nonsense about being the Maltreated Cat. He sets to work, quietly and efficiently, to bring peace to his restless master.

First, he adjusts the pillows. They must be a little higher, in order that he may curl into the crook of my arm without being squashed. Then he slightly rearranges the blankets. They must not be pulled too close or they will cause his ears to twitch, and that would disturb the therapeutical processes. After which he usually gives a faint sneeze, as a signal that the lights may now be turned out.

So we are in darkness. And 'Four' is very warm, and from his small body a strange, soothing balm is stealing. This is accompanied by the gentlest, finger-tip movement of the paws, and . . . of course . . . a slow, steady purr. The purr is regulated with the utmost art. If I stroke him, he takes this as a signal that I am not yet quite prepared for Morpheus, and the purr ascends a few notes in the scale, and is given a faint *vibrato*, suggestive of the cooing of doves. But if my hand rests beside him, slack and inert, the purr is soft-pedalled, and dies away to the faintest of sighs, which blend with the dying whispers of the wind, till all is lost in a blessed silence.

How far we have to travel before we even begin to understand the essentials of civilized comfort! One can stay at the grandest hotels, where the bedrooms are soft and sumptuous, and where the bathrooms are glittering jewel-boxes of oriental luxury. By the side of one's bed is a little contraption with buttons that ring bells to summon every sort of slave—a slave to take one's laundry, to bring a jug of ice-water, to provide an elaborate meal, to cut one's hair, to pull up the blinds, to turn down the counterpane. But there is no bell marked F, to put one in touch with the Feline Services Department. One day I should like to establish such an hotel.

However, there would be a slight but significant difference. It would be the cats who would lie in bed, pressing the bells, and the humans who would answer them.

JEALOUSY

Our drama is set on a sunny morning in the shadow of the walnut tree, and it begins with a very faint sound which you would probably not notice unless you were waiting for it—the soft whisper of fragments of walnut shell fluttering through the branches.

Down they fall, with a gentle pitter-patter, and they land at the feet of 'Five', who loftily ignores them. Rather, he pretends to ignore them, for he is sitting very still, presuming himself to be unobserved by the squirrel above. The presumption, of course, is absurd. The squirrel is fully aware of 'Five's' presence. And I am certain that he is aiming the fragments of shell directly at 'Five's' head, in a spirit of squirrelish bravado.

A swift twitch of 'Five's' tail informs me that he is beginning to be bored. One cannot sit for hours under walnut trees, being mocked, without some promise of action, and no action is pending. The squirrel, high up in the topmost branches, is surrounded by a positive bevy of walnuts; he could stay there all the morning, nibbling and spitting out those small, insulting particles. So 'Five' decides to call it a day. He yawns, stretches, and stalks forward to the trunk of the tree, on which he proceeds to sharpen his claws. He sharpens them thoroughly and methodically, with an occasional glance upwards, as though to warn the squirrel of what to expect if he continues in his outrageous conduct.

Then 'Five' turns, notices me, and promptly falls flat on his back.

As an experienced F, I correctly interpret this gesture as a sign that tummy-rubbing is demanded. 'Five's' posture is in the classic tradition; the front paws are dangling, the hind legs are slightly apart, the head is tilted to one side, there is a come-hither glint in the green eyes. The whole position has a coyness which does not quite accord with 'Five's' *embonpoint*.

But its meaning is unmistakable. Tummy-rubbing is the order of the moment. Needless to say, I obey the order.

I walk across, like an obedient slave, and set to work, supplying a variant with the under-the-chin stroke, and an occasional sharp, well-timed tweak of the tail. This demands a high standard of technique and should never be attempted except by advanced students. After a few minutes I pause, for the morning is very hot, and it is tiring work bending down.

And then, to my dismay, I notice a small black shape crouched in the door of the tool-shed. Hist . . . we are observed! 'Four', having been informed by some mystic sense that tummy-rubbing is in the air, has crept out to watch, and is regarding us with despair, grief, hatred, and a general sense of total desolation. How a small, black shape in the shadows, illuminated by only two green eyes, can convey such a complex of powerful emotions, I do not pretend to understand. But he does.

And talking of cats' eyes, is it not significant that cats are the only animals who look Man straight in the face, who are undeterred by the most arrogant human stare? If you stare at a dog the poor creature will be embarrassed, fidgeting and averting its eyes. If it were capable of blushing, it would blush. Even puppies, however gently you may speak to them, do not care for prolonged scrutiny; their reactions are much the same as those of schoolboys with a guilty conscience; it is almost as though they were plagued by a sense of original sin. If you stare at a parrot it will stare back for a little while but it is obviously none too happy about the situation, and begins to fiddle about on its perch, and turn its back and scratch its head. If you stare at a monkey its reactions are much the same as a human's. They betray embarrassment, and occasionally, particularly if they are incarcerated in a zoo, rage—which is, of course, a manifestation of fear. But cats return your gaze candidly, with no sign of perturbation. They do not blink, they do not lower their sights, the cool green eyes remain fixed on yours, making their calm appraisal. Perhaps this natural phenomenon is responsible for the phrase 'A cat may look at a queen'. In any staring match the queen would certainly be outmatched.

However, we were on the threshold of tragedy, with 'Four' in the wings, demanding instant attention. So I give a final expert stroke to 'Five's' chin and hurry over to the tool-shed. The reaction is as I expected.

'Four' immediately starts the Act. Terror is registered, and he darts away. I follow, making soothing noises. He retreats further, and then pauses looking back at me, with his head over his shoulder. If I were sensible—or if 'Four' were a dog—I should also pause, fold my arms, and say to him 'Very well, "Four", if you persist in this idiotic behaviour, that is your own affair. But if you wish to be stroked, like a good cat, you will kindly come over here and assume a stroking posture.' But I am not sensible, and 'Four' is not a dog, so I make a sudden dart, and seize him, and begin the stroking.

The technique demanded by 'Four' differs *in toto* from the technique demanded by 'Five'. The stroking must be far more robust, beginning at the back of the neck, ending at the base of the tail, and marked by a strong *vibrato*. As it increases in vigour it must be accompanied by sharp taps on the spine. If non-Fs were to observe this performance they would be confirmed in their conviction that I *am* a cat-beater, particularly as 'Four' shows his approval of them by a very peculiar blend of purrs and mews. (The reader will have guessed that 'Four', mentally and physically, has a strong streak of masochism.) However, they would be puzzled by the fact that when I stop, 'Four' makes no effort to escape, but remains there demanding more, with his behind elevated at an angle of forty-five degrees.

The stroking continues. And then, suddenly, a shadow falls on this strange scene—the shadow of a tail held very erect, coming towards us, like an accusing finger. Once again, we have been observed! I do not have to turn in order to see whose tail it is. Nor does Oscar turn as he passes, for he would not deign to cast a glance on such sickening proceedings. Scorn is written all over him . . . it is in his walk, in his whiskers, in his tail, even in his behind.

I know what he is saying to me. ' "Four" has had more than his share of back-stroking. "Five" has had more than his share of tummy-rubbing. Unless a little attention is given to *me*, there will be hell to pay.'

I know too where he is going, because the drill is always the same. He is making for the old pear tree. As soon as he reaches it, he will sniff the trunk. Then, with a single Nijinsky leap, scarcely touching the bark, he will land in the fork of the first branch, about six feet above the ground. Whereupon he will dispose himself for dalliance, with his right paw dangling languidly in front of him, ready to pounce on any prey that may present itself.

The dalliance, of course, has to be supplied by myself, and supplied quickly. So 'Four' gets a final stroke—long and lingering, to give him the idea that I am parting from him only with the greatest reluctance. And I walk across the lawn to report for duty at the pear tree.

Which shall it be? A twig? A blade of grass? An iris leaf? (I need hardly explain to Fs that I am pondering on the best form of decoy to dangle before Oscar's claws—to sweep up and down the trunk for him to pounce upon.) I pause before a cluster of lupins that have gone to seed. A lupin stick might do. The pods make an exciting rattle. But they are inclined to break off if the pounce is too energetic, leaving me only with the stump, and it is difficult to get real drama into the dalliance if one only has a stump. (An observation which, when one comes to think of it, might come more fittingly from the lips of a Manx.) Twigs, too, break off too easily, and sometimes get stuck in Oscar's teeth. It had better be the iris leaf. So I pick a nice long one—the clump is getting seriously denuded—advance to the tree, and set to work.

Up and down sweeps the iris leaf, always just out of reach of Oscar's paws. It is a moment of intense and exhausting concentration, because when you are playing this game you must project yourself into the leaf; it must be part of your own body; you must be fleeing in peril of your life. Sometimes he nearly catches me, but I am too cunning for him, I switch—via the leaf—into a crook in the pear tree, trembling, alert, and then dart up again. Oscar's tail lashes, his green eyes glisten, his sharp claws pounce and pounce again. At last, out of sheer fatigue, I let myself be caught. For a moment Oscar pretends to devour me, and then he lets the leaf fall to the ground. The dalliance is concluded. I am allowed to take my departure.

So I walk slowly back to the house, watched by three pairs of eyes. 'Four' on the lawn, 'Five' under the walnut, Oscar in the pear tree. Very different eyes, that mirror very different personalities. But those eyes have one thing in common. They are all green.

KITTENS

It will be generally agreed that babies, when compared with kittens, are very unattractive creatures.

The chief objection to babies is that they are insane. I came into the world as a lunatic and so did you, and only through a long and painful process of education did we develop into 'civilized' men and women—which means, of course, another form of lunatic, though not such a comparatively harmless one.

If we were deposited as babies on a desert island we should remain the gibbering idiots that we were at birth. Having no knowledge of any alphabet we should be unable to communicate our thoughts; indeed, we should have no thoughts to communicate; we should be guided only by the most primitive instincts. And even in these instincts we would show ourselves greatly inferior to kittens. Consider such an elementary matter as sanitation. Monkeys, the closest relatives to man in the animal kingdom, have no instinct for sanitation at all, as may be observed by paying the most cursory visit to the zoo. Our deserted babies would be equally devoid of such instincts. The smallest and wildest kitten, however, would behave impeccably; it would powder its nose and wash its hands as though it were descended from a long line of ancestors who had been accustomed to a high standard of plumbing since the days of Neanderthal man.

The doting mother, as she bends over the cradle, crooning to its bald and maniac occupant, may possibly question these observations. If she does, she can scarcely escape the charge of being non-F. Better for her to accept the truth, tuck up baby for the night, and go out to sit by the kitten basket, in order to study the behaviour of civilized young creatures.

The advent of a new kitten, in a really F household, is, or should be, a major event in the lives of all concerned. For several years a new kitten has, as it were, been hovering on my horizon, but nothing has come of it. My favourite clairvoyant, Mr Corbett, has definitely seen a kitten in his crystal ball, but he cannot forecast the date of its arrival. It is there, somewhere, in the clouds, but evidently suitable conjunction of the planets has not as yet occurred. Sometimes I suspect that this is due to the psychic influence of 'Four' and Oscar. Whenever a new kitten is being discussed, 'Four' seizes the opportunity to give a supreme performance of his role, sighing, sitting in corners, and retreating even further into the fire-place in order to cover himself in symbolic ashes. Oscar becomes more than ever clamorous for attention, and gazes at one with such an access of

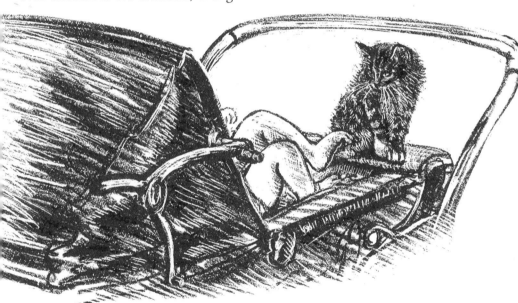

sentimentality and possessiveness that one dreads to think what would happen if he were suddenly to find a kitten on one's lap. The only person who is sensible about the whole thing is 'Five'. He has often made it clear that he would welcome some new blood in the household, and on the rare occasions when he has encountered kittens in neighbouring gardens, has given a brilliant display of kittenishness himself, in spite of his *embonpoint*.

Concerning the habits of kittens many volumes might be written ... from the time they lie suckling in the basket, pressing their small velvet paws in a gentle rhythm against their mother's breast, through those enchanted stages when they open their blue eyes which slowly turn to green, like tiny pools over which the clouds have drifted, and over the thrilling weeks in which they stagger out of the basket and gradually gain strength and grace in a series of wild adventures. There is no dull moment in all their exquisite adolescence, which would provide material for an Encyclopaedia Felinica.

In this comparatively modest work I have space for only one observation, which concerns the instinctive 'come-back' of kittens to the stimulus of danger. This is an awful subject, in the literal sense that one is filled with awe when one contemplates the miraculous delicacy of Nature's signalling system, whereby a menacing echo born on the wind can set in motion a whole complex of glandular and muscular reactions. Blake paused, in immortal astonishment, before the 'fearful symmetry' of his Tiger. I pause—though not for posterity—in equal astonishment, before the fearful symmetry of a kitten.

Watch what happens when a kitten is confronted by any potential menace, such as an unfamiliar cat. Its immediate reaction is to make itself appear larger and more formidable. And so it abruptly switches its body sideways. At the same time it arches its back and stands on tiptoe. While it is assuming this strange posture the fur rises all over its body, puffing it out and transforming its tail into the semblance of a fox's brush. Thus caparisoned—the word seems justified, for one has the feeling that the kitten is clad in a sort of ghostly armour—the kitten slowly advances.

This sequence of movements must surely be one of the most elaborate, as it is certainly one of the most beautiful, performed by any young creature in nature. Merely to describe it has made me realize how much I am missing, in my present kittenless condition. I must ring up Mr Corbett, and ask him to look once again into his crystal ball.

LAUGHTER

But not—let us be very clear about this—not what we call 'mocking laughter'. To make an animal feel ridiculous is unpardonable. This is one of the principal reasons why I loathe the circus. If a man chooses to chalk his face, paint his nose, and stand on his head, good luck to him. He may look less ludicrous in this posture than when he is strap-hanging in a bowler hat. But for God's sake let him keep his hands off the animals.

I sometimes indulge in the diversion of creating special hells for persons whom I most dislike. Among these imaginary infernos is one reserved for circus proprietors, lion-tamers, ring-masters, bull-fighters, and the like. In this arena of my dreams the audience and the animals swop places. The front stalls are filled by quantities of very beautiful lions, fanning themselves with their programmes. The dress circle is packed with an uproarious collection of dogs, of all shapes and sizes . . . a good-natured crowd, but determined to get their money's worth. The boxes are reserved for the elephants. (Sometimes, when the dream is very vivid, I give the elephants tiaras.) Prowling round at the back, tossing their manes, are the horses, looking very white and wonderful, and quite free to run out into the night as soon as they are bored.

Then the show begins. And what a show it is! The whips crack round the naked calves of the lion-tamers. (All done by kindness!) The flames leap up as the ringmasters are put through the hoop. (They really *love* it, you know!) And as a grand finale, the directors of the circus company (who have been equipped for the occasion with artificial tails) are suspended from the roof, in which position they are fed with gingerbreads soaked in rancid South African sherry. All to the uproarious applause of

the aforementioned lions, dogs, elephants, and horses . . . to say nothing of a certain rather proletarian orang-outang in the gallery and a pair of cheeky marmosets in the pit, whose behaviour is too impolite to describe in detail, even though one may sympathize with it.

Well—I have got *that* off my chest. So now we can relax, and come from the general to the particular, and focus the spotlight on to the small pink object which inspired these observations . . . Oscar's tongue.

All Fs, of course, will have delighted in those rather absurd moments when they have glanced up from a book by the fire, or paused in their knitting, to see pussy observing them, with the end of the tongue sticking out. It looks like the tip of a rose petal stuck below the nose, and pussy appears to be quite unconscious that it is out at all. You may call attention to it . . . you may say 'My dear "Four", are you aware that your tongue is sticking out?' 'Four' does not seem to hear you. You may even remark, quite severely . . . ' "Five", if you keep your tongue out like that, one day the wind will change and you will never be able to put it in again.' No heed is taken. In Oscar's case, you may even bend down and stroke him, in the hope that this will induce a change of mood and a consequent withdrawal of the tongue. It does no such thing. All that happens is that when Oscar starts to purr, as always, the purr has a faintly sibilant quality, a sort of twang, which brings back a faint echo of my childhood, when I sometimes used to put sheets of music on the open wires of our old Broadwood piano, to simulate a guitar. The tongue remains out.

And it really is—let's face it—rather funny.

But I am quite sure that we should not laugh at it—not, at least, in pussy's face. The tongue-protruding is a symbol of peace and contentment and trust and affection. One does not sit for long periods on a mat with one's tongue out, gazing with swimming eyes at somebody at least ten times larger than oneself, if one is in any immediate anxiety about one's personal security.

And yet, one *wants* to laugh. The trouble, of course, is anthropomorphic; it arises from our terrible habit of translating animal habits into human terms. If, for example, we found ourselves in a box at the opera in the company of an exquisite female and if, during one of the *longueurs* of

Siegfried we found that the delicious creature was regarding us from under her languorous lashes with a small, pointed cerise tongue protruding from her lips, we might well be excused for suspecting that some peculiar form of badinage was being suggested. In which case, we would react according to our temperaments. My own reaction would almost certainly be a swift exit to the bar.

I am not absolutely certain—for after all one is something of a pioneer in these problems—of the ultimate F ruling in this dilemma: of what, in short, the F should actually *do*—though I rather suspect, while emphasizing that I am speaking without the Book, no true and authoritative Book as yet being in existence (and I trust that the reader will forgive this parody, however momentarily, of Henry James, whom let us salute in passing as F from tip to toe) . . . I rather suspect that the *true* F, the ideal F, the shiningly impeccable F, would put his tongue out too.

One day, I am going to try it. I shall be sitting at my desk, writing beautiful thoughts, and I shall look across the room and there by the fire will be Oscar, lying on his back, with his front paws dangling before him, gazing at me with his tongue out. And I shall lay down my pen, and put my tongue out too. And neither of us will laugh.

MILK

I have just been watching 'Five' drink his milk. It is a curious operation, for he does not really drink it at all. He stands in front of it, and then, very languidly, produces a paw which he dips in the milk. He proceeds to lick the paw, with a faintly supercilious expression, as though he were savouring a vintage wine.

One is reminded of a French marquise dipping sponge-cakes into green Chartreuse under the chandeliers of Versailles. I doubt if there is any historical authority for suggesting that French marquises ever did anything so vulgar, even in 1788, but it is the sort of thing that one remembers from childhood readings of Carlyle and *A Tale of Two Cities*.

'Five', in spite of his mixed origin and the cockney smudge on his nose, has an aura of aristocracy. If he had lived in the eighteenth century he could have outstared any French marquise, even the Comtesse de Polignac. He is so fussy that on the flight to Varennes he would have been a considerable encumbrance; but if I had had anything to do with it, he would have been given the best seat.

(Pause for thought. Was Marie Antoinette F? My instinctive retort to this question is 'No'. I feel that she probably drifted about with rather raffish borzois who would have been the better for a good scrubbing. Though, once again, I have no historical authority for this suggestion. Danton, most certainly, was F, and so was Robespierre, though he was very wicked and scratchy, and up-to-no-good around the railings of the Palais Royal. A great deal of human misery might have been averted if Robespierre had been 'arranged'. But that, after all, might be said of most of the great 'heroes' of history, from Alexander onwards.)

To return to 'Five' and his milk—for I must constantly remind

65

myself that this is intended to be a serious work, destined for the shelves of eminent veterinary surgeons.

One of the most common delusions of the non-F world is that every cat likes milk, and that if only they have enough of it, all will be well. But all cats do *not* like milk. Consider my own little family. 'Five' as we have seen regards milk as an aperitif. 'Four' scarcely regards it at all. He prefers water—of which, needless to say, there is always a bowl under the sink. Occasionally, after eating his fish, he will stalk past the milk saucer and then pause, glance over his shoulder, and—if anybody is watching—heave a deep sigh, retrace his steps, and take a few timid sips.

But 'Four's' favourite beverage, when he is allowed it, is soda water, and I think that this must be due to the streak of Siamese in him. I originally encountered this curious taste for soda water in my Siamese cat 'One', now alas departed from this world. He was first attracted to it, obviously, by his discovery that soda water syphons frequently leaked, making strange hissing noises, and producing drops which trembled on the tips of the spouts—drops which must be attended to, and dabbed at. Many is the time that I have come into the dining-room to find 'One' dabbing at the drops, with a little pool of soda water forming beneath the syphon, spoiling the veneer. After a while I began to grow suspicious. Surely the syphons were becoming less and less efficient? Surely it was strange that so many of them should be leaking like this? And then, one day, I caught him in the act, with his paw on the handle, giving it a series of sharp dabs

to make it work. After which, the syphons were placed in a less accessible position, and the table gradually regained its veneer.

'Four' has not resorted to such knavish tricks. However, he gets his soda water all the same, for he always seems to know when it is being used. He likes it at its fizziest, and he drinks it from a saucer, giving an occasional sneeze when a bubble goes up his nose.

But we were speaking of milk.

The only inveterate milk-drinker in my family is Oscar, who absorbs it like a sponge. Every morning, as soon as I have been presented with the breakfast tray, Oscar puts his head through the door, steps forward, and leaps on to the bed. He has come for his milk, but he is a stickler for etiquette and he knows that certain ceremonial procedures must first be observed before he actually demands it. First, he must give a sharp swish to my letters, sending them on to the floor. Next, he must sit on the *Daily Telegraph*, and—if possible—so disarrange it that I shall be unable to read the leader. He would not like me to be depressed by its sombre tone. Finally, he must have a little organ practice, pressing his paws up and down with great fervour on the keys (my ankles) and gazing at me, and through me, with such an intensity of musical emotion that I can almost hear the strains of the Lost Chord.

He is now ready for his milk, which I pour out in a saucer on the tray . . . thinking, as I do so, how wonderful it would be, for once in a way, to be able to drink a cup of coffee with a saucer attached, instead of having to drink it out of a cup with no saucer, as though one were at Waterloo Station.

But that is an unworthy thought. For these milk-drinking moments are really among the happiest of my rather muddled life. The day is young, the house is quiet, the telephone has not yet begun to ring. Through my window I can see the massive branches of the old walnut tree, which time has moulded into a design of strong masculine beauty—one is reminded of muscled arms delighting in the exercise of their strength. And here, on the warm bed, bending over the tray, drinking his milk, is Oscar. The pink tongue darts in and out, making the pleasantest little splashing sound, the eyes are half closed in contentment, gradually the level of the milk sinks till the saucer is dry, and the splashing sound is replaced by two or three faintly rasping noises as he makes sure that the saucer is quite clean. After which, he sits up very straight, sniffs, and begins to wash his face, as all good cats should.

He is happy, I am happy, the whole world seems to be purring. Then the telephone starts to ring. And as I struggle out of bed to answer it I think how strange it is that we should spend our lives sweating and striving for this and that and the other when all we need is here at hand. A cat, a saucer of milk, a few blankets, and through the window the glimpse of a walnut tree lifting its limbs in delight to the clean, cold sky.

NEIGHBOURS

Was Ham Common an F district? This was, of course, the first thing I wished to know when I was moving in.

To inquire of the house-agents would have been useless, as I knew from long experience. House-agents tell you everything except what you really want to know. Invariably they inform you that there is a 'wealth of old oak'. Never that there is a wealth of old cats.

By an F district I mean a district where on one's afternoon walks through the little Georgian streets that cluster by the river one would be privileged to see plump creatures sitting on doorsteps, and—by employing various cunning devices, such as twig-rattling, and key-jingling—entice them into a short session of general conversation. (These interludes are not always so tranquil as they sound. Sometimes the curtains of the house are drawn, and an angry woman looks out, with drawn brows, convinced that one is a cat-stealer.) I also mean a district where, while one is strolling in the shadow of a high garden wall, one may suddenly hear a strange, unearthly wail and—looking up—discover that Providence has provided one with a Siamese. Indeed, there is just such a walk in my neighbourhood, and I often wander past it in the hope that the resident Siamese may appear. But it seldom does so, and up till now it has remained regrettably aloof, not to say snooty. Part of the trouble is that the top of the wall is just too high for me to reach it. If it were lower I could startle it with a brilliant display of back-slappings and reverse whisker-strokings, at the same time murmuring, in a casual manner, that I happened to be the President of the Bexhill-on-Sea Cat Club, and that I was generally well thought of in the feline world. It gives me no opportunity to convey this information, and as far as it is concerned I might be nobody at all.

However, there are other feline neighbours, who are not so backward—and though it may seem outrageous to suggest that there could be *any* time in the life of a true F when the visits of *any* cat could be unwelcome—I must reluctantly confess that there have been moments when the visits of these neighbours have been embarrassing.

Which brings us to the Strange Case of 'Five' and The Toms.

This is a delicate matter.

For the trouble about 'Five' is that owing to his extreme prettiness, his bar-maid plumpness, and the way he rolls his enormous green eyes, he puts quite the wrong ideas into the heads of the more rakish toms who roam the district. This results in situations of some difficulty. 'Five's' attitude is completely innocent; he is inviting no irregular responses; he is merely intrigued by the singular antics and caterwaulings of the large fierce creatures who come and serenade him. What can they possibly *mean*, these hoarse entreaties? Why all this fuss? These are the questions he asks himself, as he sits in all his plumpness and prettiness, rolling his eyes, within safe distance of the haven of the cat-door.

What does one do, in these circumstances? One cannot go out and read them the Wolfenden Report, because they would not understand it, and even if they did, it might only make matters worse. One cannot rush out and start shouting and throwing things, because any such behaviour would immediately be interpreted by 'Five', with his ultra-sensitive nature, as a reproach to himself, and he would only dart off and cower under a rhododendron, in a state of maidenly alarm. Which, in its turn, would probably inspire the toms with even more inflammatory notions.

What, in fact, I do is—talk. Casting a look of grave reproof at the tom, I lift up 'Five' and take him indoors, and sit him down and read him a quiet lecture. 'My dear "Five",' I begin . . . but it would sound too idiotic if I were to put it into direct speech. The general purport is that he has led a very sheltered life, that this is a changing world, in which nothing is quite the same as it was, and in which people, and cats, often behave in a way which would have made our grandmothers turn in their graves. No blame, I assure him, attaches to anybody. Even the tom, if visited by a

psychiatrist, would probably be informed that its behaviour was due to some quite common complex. All the same ... my dear 'Five' ... a simple life is usually happier than a complex one, so next time you see these serenading gentlemen, do not roll your eyes at them. Just look the other way.

Apart from these problems, life goes by placidly enough, with only just enough drama to lend a spice of variety to the feline calendar. Our two nearest neighbours are Rudolph and Webster, in the cottage next door. Rudolph is ginger, with a temper to match—a most peppery creature, though I hate to say it. We hardly know him, except as an orange streak, darting up the trunks of pear trees or shooting across the lawn, with a tail inflated like a fox's brush. Whenever Rudolph appears there is trouble.

Webster, on the other hand, is the gentlest of cats—a soft brown tabby with melting eyes. It says a great deal for the sweetness of his disposition that 'Four', 'Five', and Oscar have allowed him the freedom of the cat-door. No, perhaps that would be putting it too strongly; but at least they make no active protest when he appears. The drill is always the same. There is the sound of a 'plonk' outside as Webster jumps down from the low roof of the tool-shed. A shadow falls across the cat-door. 'Four', 'Five', and Oscar, sitting with folded arms round the fire, exchange Looks. The cat-door creaks, as a brown paw is pushed through; there is a moment's pause, and then Webster's head appears, followed by his body. He gives a faint mew and then walks calmly—followed by the Looks—to the fish-plates under the sink, and proceeds to eat what is left. When I first saw this phenomenon I could hardly believe my eyes; cats are usually bitterly jealous of any violation of their domestic territory.

Webster is a car-sitter. On summer mornings, when I have left the car outside the garden gate over-night, I draw the curtains and look out, and there is Webster, stretched on the bonnet, basking in the sunshine. I have never fully understood this penchant, shared by so many cats, for the bonnets of cars. In cold weather, if a car had just been driven, there would be an obvious explanation—the warmth of the bonnet. But cats sit on cars in all weathers; never in my experience *in* them, of their own free will, though I believe that Siamese cats can be trained to do so.

Webster is also a post-sitter. He perches on one of the posts of the garden gate, and as he is very fat, with a large sit-upon, and as the post is very slender, he overlaps, so that he gives a strange effect of being impaled. How he manages to retain his balance in such a posture is a mystery.

From these brief notes it will be gathered that Webster has definitely come to stay.

And then there are 'Omo', 'Daz', and 'Tide'.

These are three snow-white kittens who have only recently come into my life. Perhaps it is not quite accurate to describe them as 'neighbours', because they live on the other side of the common, in a cottage so small that when the last white tail has vanished through the front-door you feel that the interior must be seriously overcrowded. The cottage belongs to an old lady whom some of my readers may have met before—Miss Mint.

Miss Mint is one of those gentle, unassuming women who always seem to attract to themselves the most extraordinary adventures. If there is a crook in the neighbourhood—and even in this predominantly Jane

Austen locality crooks have been known to intrude—he makes straight for Miss Mint, and either borrows money or sells her something that does not work. If Borstal boys escape from homes of correction they make a bee-line over Miss Mint's fence. And if illegitimate babies are being deposited on local doorsteps, they are invariably deposited on Miss Mint. No . . . I must not exaggerate. But since her arrival at the cottage, five years ago, there have been two such unexpected infants, one in a fully fledged pram and the other in a cardboard box, which is quite enough for a maiden lady with a taste for water-colours.

And if kittens are being abandoned . . . but here again I must not exaggerate, for it has only happened once. The circumstances were such as would have appealed to any Victorian melodramatist. It was Christmas Eve; it was bitter cold, with a flurry of snow dusting the top of the laurel hedge; and there, on the doorstep, when Miss Mint returned from church, was a wicker laundry basket with the three white kittens. And lest your heart is wrung by the thought of them, shivering and deserted, they were reposing on an old plaid shawl wrapped round a hot water bottle, which was still warm.

I do not know enough about these three small bundles of enchantment, as yet, to recount any of their adventures. At the moment all I can say is that they are living up to their names in an uncanny manner, thereby justifying my theory that a name has a strange creative force of its own, which gradually imposes upon its owner a sort of psychic personality. If you have a female infant, and if you are so unkind as to baptize it Clara, a form of Clara it will become, which can hardly be any nice girl's ambition.

In the case of the kittens, 'Omo' really *does* 'add brightness to whiteness'; he is by far the perkiest. 'Daz' really *does* 'wash whitest of all'; at least, he washes longest, which in the case of a kitten is much the same thing. And 'Tide' is aptly named because this excellent detergent, as we all know, is blended with the mystic 'Bluinite'—a compound which for some reason or other I cannot discover in the Oxford Dictionary—and you can distinctly see specks of Bluinite in 'Tide's' eyes.

So there are our neighbours. Not a very large cast, I am afraid, but large enough. For a single cat, by the mystic force of its personality, can fill the largest stage.

ODES

Most of the poets who have written verse about cats would have been better employed composing advertisements for detergents. Even Keats, in his sonnet 'To Mrs Reynolds's Cat' was only able to achieve a patronizing sneer:

> For all the wheezy asthma—and for all
> Thy tail's tip is nick'd off—and though the fists
> Of many a maid have given thee many a maul,
> Still is that fur as soft as when the lists
> In youth thou enter'dst on glass-bottled wall.

These lamentable lines stamp the author of the 'Ode to a Nightingale', for all time, as non-F. They are as cacophonous as any of the grunts coughed up by the spluttering pen of Robert Browning. Apart from that, they have a streak of insensitivity that mounts almost to sadism. Unless, of course, you think that the painful disease of asthma, in man or beast, is a fit subject for satire, or that there is anything amusing about the idea of young females 'mauling' defenceless animals.

Shelley was almost as bad. His 'Verses on a Cat' are so crude and ugly that they might have been written by the school bully. Wordsworth, by comparison, was almost F—there is a feline lilt and grace about his lines 'The Kitten and Falling Leaves'; but he gives himself away in the last five lines:

> What would little Tabby care
> For the plaudits of the crowd?
> Over-happy to be proud
> Over-wealthy in the treasure
> Of her own exceeding pleasure?

75

No F could have written those words. Little Tabby would have cared a great deal for the plaudits of the crowds. Of all animals cats are most conscious of their audience, and always give their best performances before a full house.

But the cat-poets reach their lowest level when they begin to symbolize, when they invest Felinity with ancient rites, mysteries, and what-have-you. One of the worst poems ever written, surely, must be Oscar Wilde's 'The Sphinx'. Listen to this:

> *Lift up your large black satin eyes which are like cushions where one sinks!*
> *Fawn at my feet, fantastic Sphinx! and sing me all your memories!*

No, Oscar, *no*! Cross it out, and throw it away, and call a hansom cab and take Lord Alfred out to luncheon at the Café Royal . . . where, perhaps, after the third absinthe, you will say something delicious about the ortolans.

'*Cushions where one sinks*' indeed! Could the Rhyming Dictionary suggest no happier echo than that? The picture evoked by these words would have made an enchanting subject for Max; Wilde was a very heavy man and a great many cushions would have been necessary. As for 'fawning at his feet'—or rather at his side-buttoned, patent leather boots —never did the artful aids of alliteration lead an artist so astray. Even the humblest kitten from the alley would be outraged by an invitation to 'fawn'. Really, one would think that dear Oscar had been keeping company with corgis.

But sometimes, out of all this welter of inferior rhyming, a master-piece emerges. Such is Thomas Hardy's 'Last Words to a Dumb Friend'— an elegy more moving than many that have been carved on the tombs of princes. And Swinburne, in his verses 'To a Cat', wrote as if he were addressing a creature of equal, though different, intelligence.

And here and there, as one thumbs the pages of feline literature, a little gleaming phrase shines out, like cats' eyes gleaming in the dark.

Wind is a cat
That prowls at night
Now in a valley
Now on a height
It sings to the moon
It scratches at doors;
It lashes its tail
Around chimneys and roars
Then chasing the stars
To the tops of the firs
Curls down for a nap
And purrs, and purrs.

I know nothing about the poet who created that charming conceit —Ethel Romig Fuller. But we will all agree that she was definitely F.

And so was another American—Helen Maring. She it was who wrote a poem which might be called 'the humblest poem ever written' ...so tiny, so naïve, that it lives only through the virtue of its own humility. Why does it move me so? Listen:

I have no pets to hold my heart
No pets to fill a need:
But hungry creatures of the night
Come to my porch to feed . . .
No litter in the puppy's bed
No cat beside the fire,
Only the friends I do not see
To fill the deep desire.
The city's poor and hungry cats
Whose masters know the need.
I have no pets to hold my heart—
But little friends to feed.

Poetry? Perhaps not. Does it matter so much? For there is something greater than poetry, and that is compassion, which is the poetry of the human heart.

And yet, there *should* be great cat poetry. There should be triumphant Odes to Tabbies; there should be Sonnets to the Siamese; there should be Epics to the Unknown Heroes of the Alley.

Could we not write one ourselves? Could we not, for example, sit down at this very moment and write an ode to Oscar? Would it be so very difficult? After all, words are words, and one is used to adjusting them, and if one is presented with the extra puzzle of a rhyme, that should but add spice to the exercise. Even as I write, Oscar enters, rather solemnly, sits by the side of the waste-paper basket, and gazes up at me. I look into his eyes. So it shall be a poem to Oscar's eyes. We look at each other. I write . . .

> In your eyes is a strange sea-changing
> Green to gold and gold to grey,
> Dark and swift as the west wind ranging
> Over the breakers in the bay . . .
> In your eyes there are ancient sorrows
> Tears unshed for tales forlorn
> Tales of all our lost tomorrows
> All our yesterdays unborn.
> In your eyes . . .

But no; a cobbler should stick to his last. It is sorry stuff. And yet, four words in that little jingle set me thinking, as though somebody else had written them. Our 'lost tomorrows' . . . our 'yesterdays unborn'. There is something there, some elusive truth that might be worth pursuing. There *are* tomorrows that may be lost . . . dawns on which we deliberately draw down the blinds. There are yesterdays, in which we live and have our being, though they never happened at all. It is all very confusing. Maybe a true poet could tell me what I am trying to say.

Oscar knows, of course. But Oscar is keeping his own counsel.

POWER

'Power tends to corrupt and absolute power corrupts absolutely.' LORD ACTON

This sombre generalization has been quoted so often before that you may wonder why I should quote it again, particularly in these light-hearted pages. It has been the theme of countless essays for schoolboys and undergraduates. In the 'thirties, during the rise of Hitler and Mussolini, it was set up in permanent type in the offices of our great newspapers. The leader-writers would have been lost without it.

But always it has been applied to *men*. It has been used as a sort of yardstick to measure the pace of a dictator's decadence. A very efficient yardstick it has proved to be, historically; with its assistance you can trace the gradual hardening of the lines in a 'great' man's face, the slow, cruel ossification of the hands that hold the reins of authority.

Nobody, as far as I am aware, has yet applied this grim truth to the relationship of man with the animal kingdom. It is about time that somebody did so.

Consider an extreme example—the lion-tamer in the circus, an institution which I have attacked before and shall attack again. This is probably bad policy for any writer; not only does he incur the displeasure of one of the most powerful vested interests in the entertainment industry but he invites the attention of a very special brand of animal lunatic. I know this from bitter experience. Whenever I have breathed a word of criticism of circuses, shoals of protesting letters have arrived. 'But the elephants *love* being made to stand on their heads! And the dear little dogs *adore* being made to walk the tight rope in pink silk trousers with a spot-light in the eyes, night after night! And the ponies would feel positively *miserable* if they were just running round the fields instead of waltzing backwards in front of a deafening brass band! As for the lions . . .'

Let us get back to those lions and the men who put them through their paces. Let us see this beastly business in its true light.

A lion is a cat. A very large cat, that has the power of inflicting death on a man.

Death can only be matched by death, and that—when all the trimmings are off—is the basis of the lion-tamer's little game. He makes the lion perform, for profit, under the constant threat of death. And the lion knows it. He is reminded of it by a thousand prods and insults and cuts and lashes. He roars his protests, he makes clumsy, futile gestures with his giant paws, there is a blazing grief in his tormented eyes, but he goes through with the act. Because he does not want to die. Even in the glaring lights, amid this bewildering uproar, subjected to a physical and psychological torture that makes the methods of the Gestapo seem comparatively humane, he is still alive, and life is sweet, or could be. And for that reason, and for that reason only, he does not leap off his stool and hurl himself in a single lethal avenging blow at the ugly little puppet who has taken command of his life.

Anybody who denies these obvious—and to me, very moderate—arguments, should have his head examined. And even more, his heart. The circus is an institution which should long ago have vanished from any enlightened society, and the profession of lion-taming should long ago have been abolished by law, together with such comparatively respectable callings as drug-peddling and white slavery.

There we go again! Getting all hot under the collar, when really we only set out to amuse. Which is why no work of mine will ever be what the critics call an 'artistic unity'.

To relieve the tension, let us leave the stench and uproar of these vicious places, and return to the quiet green lawn. And let us reduce the scale of the picture, and turn the lion into a cat. The lesson is still the same, even if it is in terms of comedy instead of tragedy.

Can you imagine calling a cat to 'heel'? One's mind boggles at the prospect. Supposing I were walking across the lawn with 'Five', and I suddenly called 'Heel,' what would happen? 'Five' would stop in his tracks and very slowly turn his head, and regard me with an expression of the utmost astonishment. What *was* that strange word? And to whom was it addressed? If he were in an amiable mood, the look of astonishment would be tempered by pity. Perhaps I am feeling unwell? Perhaps the sound 'heel' . . . unless he misinterpreted it . . . was some strange form of human hiccup? If that were the case, his natural kindness, and feline etiquette, instructs him to ignore it. And so, with a faint shrug, he would resume his walk, holding his tail very erect, in the assured conviction that where *he* leads, I will follow.

This seems to me precisely as it should be. It is the only proper relationship between a human being and an animal. Anybody . . . but *anybody* . . . any lout, any half-wit, any scruffy, self-centred moron, can command the affection and the servile obedience of a dog, but it takes intelligence and understanding—sometimes I think a certain psychic rapport—to win the affection of a cat. As for obedience, you will never get it, and if you are even faintly worthy of the honourable title of F, you will never want it. This is probably the root difference between those who are 'pro-dog' or 'pro-cat'. I am 'pro' practically anything on four legs except snakes, which is perhaps not quite how I meant to put it, but we will let it stand. But the reason why I and my fellow Fs tend more to the feline than the canine is basically because we have a greater respect for the whole animal kingdom.

In case this makes a number of tweedy ladies snort with such loud indignation that their corgis rise from the hearth-rug in dismay and take refuge in the gun-room—I am assuming that such barbaric strongholds still exist—let me ask them a question. Have they never felt even a faint shiver of disquiet at the sight of a man with a well-trained dog? A nice young man in tweeds, with a pipe and a good pair of calves, going for a walk across the common with a pedigree Alsatian? Does such a spectacle arouse no feelings of alarm and despondency? Do they see it all from the outside, as a simple picture of normal outdoor English life?

I don't. And in case the tweedy ones think that this must indicate some form of moral perversity, let them look at the picture through my eyes.

There he goes, our young man with the Alsatian, and how bravely he struts along with the dog frisking beside him! How proudly he holds his head, with this comical slave at his side!

But then, he nears the main road. Suddenly, things are different. He snaps 'Heel.' And the dog, if it is a good dog, comes to heel. But as it does so, it cringes, with its tail between its legs. It is a good dog, a well-treated dog, fed on the best biscuits, tended by the best vet, adored by the family. And no doubt the young man is a good young man, as straight as a die, a faithful husband, a loving father, with all the approved instincts. One of the best.

The fact remains that the relationship between him and his dog is a slave relationship, and is *ipso facto* corrupt. If I were to read this statement to the Canine Committee of the local Rotary Club there would probably be a great deal of raising of hairy eyebrows.

And now the tweedy ones can go off to their gun-rooms, and extract their corgis from behind their husbands' macintoshes, where they will doubtless be cowering, and take the ecstatic creatures for a walk. But when they call their dogs to 'heel', I hope that they will not snap the word with quite such assurance, as though they had a divine right to use it, merely because they have two legs instead of four. It is not a pretty word and what it stands for is in no way commendable. Lord Acton knew what he was talking about.

QUIZ

All conscientious Fs from time to time should do a little mental stock-taking, in order to assure themselves that they are not growing lax, and that their standards are not slipping. The following simple test will help them to assess their own qualifications correctly. It is composed on the familiar lines of the popular quiz game, which is usually devoted to less important subjects.

Each question has four alternative answers, and each answer is marked with a corresponding letter, A, B, C, or D. These letters entitle you to certain marks—3, 2, 1, or 0. Take a sheet of paper, and answer questions with complete honesty, writing down your various As, Bs, Cs, or Ds. Then turn to the end of the chapter, where you will find what each answer is worth in terms of marks. Add them all up, and you will find your correct F category.

I hope that the above paragraph makes sense; I have been tying myself up in knots for the past half-hour, trying to make it clear. Arithmetic was never my strong point.

Here goes:

1. *If you are lunching alone on casserole of chicken, and if pussy enters the room at precisely the moment when you remove the lid—as she almost certainly will—what do you do?*

A. Shoo her away?

B. Extract a piece of chicken, put it on a side-plate, cut it up, blow on it—in a genteel fashion—and then present it to pussy?

C. Mix some gravy with some bread and put it aside to cool?

D. Take out a small portion, such as a giblet, and place it before pussy on the carpet?

2. *If pussy is lost, what do you do?*

(In asking this question I am assuming that you live in surroundings where there is at least some access to the outside world, even if it is only over the wall into your neighbour's back garden. Also that pussy has been lost for at least six hours.)

A. Ring up the police?

B. Stand at the back door calling 'Puss puss'?

C. Patrol the district with a tin plate, tapping it with a fork to simulate a dinner gong, at the same time ringing your neighbours' doorbells to inquire if they have seen a tabby with a smudge on its nose?

D. Trust in God and read Psalm 23?

3. *If pussy is sick on the carpet, what do you do?*

A. Ring the bell for Gaskin?

B. Clear it up with a shovel and when you next meet pussy, greet her with a scowl?

C. Clear it up with last week's copy of the *News of the World*, sigh, and when you next meet pussy greet her with a sympathetic smile and a stroke, but only a very tentative one, in case she might do it again on the linoleum?

D. Examine the unpleasant evidence, for traces of fur or other irritants, clear it up, go out into the larder to sniff the fish saucepan, and . . . if the results of these tests are negative . . . make a note on your pad to ring up the vet?

4. *If you are visited by a non-F friend who dislikes cats, what do you do?*

(I don't mean a person who has a genuine neurasthenic cat-phobia —merely somebody who shoos them away.)

A. Do you politely remove pussy from the room?

B. Do you endeavour to reason with the non-F, informing her that cats are really 'just as intelligent or devoted as dogs'?

C. Do you allow things to take their course, in the faintly malicious hope that pussy may spring on the non-F's lap?

D. Do you keep pussy firmly on your own lap, and ask the non-F if she would be so kind as to pour out the tea?

5. *If pussy is fighting another pussy, what do you do?*
   A. Ring for Gaskin and rush upstairs for the aspirin?
   B. Shout and roar and hurl small clods of earth?
   C. Intervene at all costs, even if it means climbing into the next garden?
   D. Nothing?

6. *If pussy refuses to eat her fish, what do you do?*
   (I am assuming, of course, that the fish is fresh and that pussy's nose is cold and her fur is in good shape and that there are no signs of physical or mental indisposition.)
   A. Speak to her severely, telling her that she will get no more until she has eaten this lot?
   B. Put the fish on a clean plate, rearrange it in a different pattern, and then take pussy for a walk in the garden in the hope that nature will eventually take its course?
   C. Cook another lot of fish?
   D. Open a tin of cat's meat?

So much for the questions. Now for the answers. The maximum score is 18, so anything above 15 may be regarded as excellent. From 15 to 12 is quite good. From 12 to 9 is doubtful. Below 9 is beyond hope.

	A	B	C	D
Question 1	0	3	1	2
Question 2	1	2	3	0
Question 3	1	0	2	3
Question 4	3	0	1	2
Question 5	1	2	3	0
Question 6	0	3	2	1

I trust that most Fs will agree with the marks that I have assigned to their answers. However, there are two cases in which there may perhaps be some grounds for argument.

The first is in question 4, which deals with the problem of what to do when visited by a non-F. I have given top marks to the person who 'politely removes pussy from the room'. This may seem an unwarranted surrender to non-Fness, but as the result of long and earnest consideration I have decided that this is the best course. The non-F will only bore pussy, and pussy will make the non-F feel ill at ease.

After all, in our dealings with non-Fs we must never forget that their non-Fness is not their own fault; they were just made that way. It is an affliction rather than a crime, and we must always be very nice to them.

Speak to non-Fs gently and always open the door for them when they leave the room—which one hopes they will do as soon as possible. If the subject of Fness crops up, brush it aside, as one would if an unmusical person were to express an opinion about Bach.

The other marking which may be contested is 3 for B in question 6—about putting the fish on a clean plate, rearranging it in a different pattern, and then taking pussy for a walk in the garden. Some Fs may consider that the award should more properly have gone to C—'Cook another lot of fish.' But I feel very strongly that B is right.

It is a question of feline psychology. Granted that pussy is in good health, that the fish is fresh and served at the proper time, the reason for pussy's refusal to eat is almost certainly psychological. For instance, at precisely the moment when she was about to take the first bite, the dustman may have clattered past, causing alarm and creating a temporary complex. Or there may have been some disturbing domestic incident such as the changing of a piece of furniture. We may, perhaps, have moved her armchair to another part of the room without previously consulting her, and this she naturally finds very strange behaviour and not at all the thing; she must express her disapproval in some way or other. People must learn. The fish must be loftily ignored.

All such temporary upsets can quickly be cured by a walk in the garden, accompanied by tactful strokings and twiddlings of twigs. By the time we return to the kitchen, where the newly arranged fish is waiting on a clean plate, pussy will almost certainly have regained her appetite.

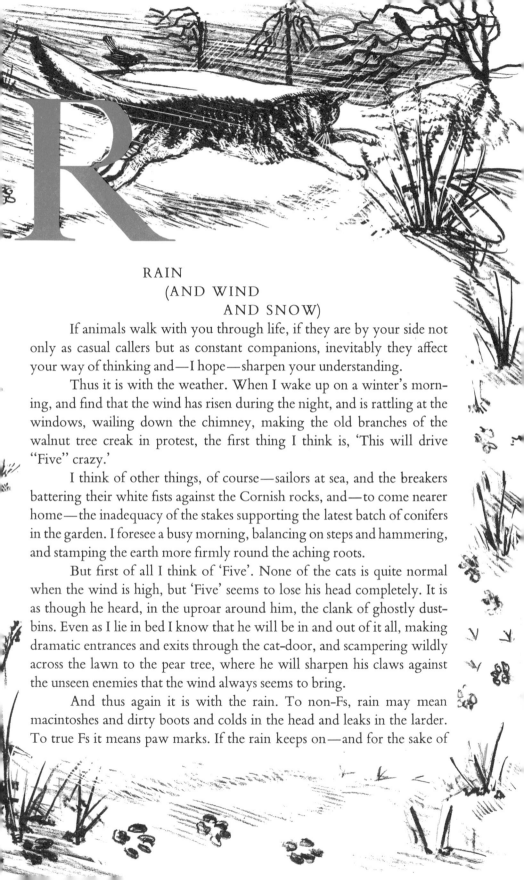

RAIN
(AND WIND
AND SNOW)

If animals walk with you through life, if they are by your side not only as casual callers but as constant companions, inevitably they affect your way of thinking and—I hope—sharpen your understanding.

Thus it is with the weather. When I wake up on a winter's morning, and find that the wind has risen during the night, and is rattling at the windows, wailing down the chimney, making the old branches of the walnut tree creak in protest, the first thing I think is, 'This will drive "Five" crazy.'

I think of other things, of course—sailors at sea, and the breakers battering their white fists against the Cornish rocks, and—to come nearer home—the inadequacy of the stakes supporting the latest batch of conifers in the garden. I foresee a busy morning, balancing on steps and hammering, and stamping the earth more firmly round the aching roots.

But first of all I think of 'Five'. None of the cats is quite normal when the wind is high, but 'Five' seems to lose his head completely. It is as though he heard, in the uproar around him, the clank of ghostly dust-bins. Even as I lie in bed I know that he will be in and out of it all, making dramatic entrances and exits through the cat-door, and scampering wildly across the lawn to the pear tree, where he will sharpen his claws against the unseen enemies that the wind always seems to bring.

And thus again it is with the rain. To non-Fs, rain may mean macintoshes and dirty boots and colds in the head and leaks in the larder. To true Fs it means paw marks. If the rain keeps on—and for the sake of the aforesaid conifers we may well hope that it does—there will be paw marks all over the house. On the window-sills, round the fish plates under the sink, in the bath, on the draining board, and—of course—firmly printed across the papers on my desk. Fs do not resent these paw marks; on the contrary, they welcome them. If I were the sort of person who wrote for posterity, I might harbour flattering thoughts about those paw marks, picturing the puzzlement of some critic unborn as he bent over these ghostly symbols, bespattering the dusty pages. However, I have often had a notion that the authors who court the critics of tomorrow have seldom been kindly received by the critics of today. Present popularity, whatever the intelligentsia may say to the contrary, is not always the prelude to future oblivion.

None of this is very apposite to the theme which we are developing, so let us content ourselves by noting that my own manuscripts go straight into the waste-paper basket, Oscar's paw marks and all.

Cats even invest a fall of snow with an extra magic. The afternoon grows chill and sullen, the skies darken before their time, and in the air is the curious scent that means snow is on its way. On the following morning one looks out of the window on to the exquisite transformation scene which—though I am old enough to know better—never fails to give me the same sort of thrill as one had at one's first pantomime, when the curtain rose on a stage glittering white, with a diamond palace whose towers reached up to a sky ablaze with silver sequins.

As soon as breakfast is over one wraps up and pulls on gum-boots, filled with excitement at the thought of all that is waiting in the Arctic world outside. The camellias will be the first port of call, in order that the

weight of snow may be shaken from their branches; there was once a sad occasion when one of my best camellias was split clean in half after a heavy fall. Then we must go to the tool-shed for a long broom, and over to the greenhouse to scrape the snow from the roof. This, I freely admit, I do for the sheer fun of it. There is something oddly satisfactory about scraping snow from a greenhouse roof, hearing it 'plonk' down to the earth, and watching the inside of the greenhouse, which had been cloaked and shadowed, come back to life as the sun floods in again through the clear glass. Yes, it will be an exciting morning.

But look! As we step out of the porch, relishing the crunch of snow beneath our feet, which is unlike any other sound in nature, we see that somebody has been here before us—in fact, several somebodies. Three sets of paw prints start at the base of the walnut tree and then fan out to the north, the east and the west. On this immaculate surface they have a carven delicacy, as though the cats had been treading with special care and elegance. How wonderful it would be to shrink, to become small and furry, to find oneself in the proud possession of a tail, and to start stalking those prints! Each of them, we may be sure, could tell a tale of adventure.

Indeed, even as we stand there staring we shall find that if we let our eyes follow the track leading to the north it will conduct us to the old pear tree. And there, high up in the fork, is 'Five'.

He is looking madder than ever, with his ears at the alert, and his fur fluffed out against the cold, and he is turning his head this way and that as though he had never seen a fall of snow before. Usually when any of the cats is stationed in the fork of the pear tree it is a sign that dalliance is demanded, and one must go in search of leaves and twigs to twiddle before them. Not today. All one's efforts would be ignored; there are too many counter-attractions, highlighted by the snow. The occasional blackbird, making his swift staccato progress across the dazzling white, looks bigger and blacker than ever before, and the tracks he leaves, like carelessly scribbled phrases of music, must be terribly tantalizing. And then, with each breath of the wind, a little flurry of snowflakes flutters down from the upper branches, and to 'Five', dabbing at them with his paw, they must seem like the white petals that he chases over the lawn in the winds of June, or the white butterflies that he stalks in summer as they hover over the purple panicles of the buddleia.

The snow and the storm, the sun and the shadow, the wind and the rain . . . these can mean little to the city dweller, imprisoned in his concrete tomb; to the countryman they are a dominating theme in the whole pattern of his existence. And to the countryman who is also an F, the Theme has infinite variations.

SOLITUDE

A sad section, this.

Last night I had to go to the opera. There I was at seven o'clock, all dressed up in the hall, looking into the mirror and tucking in my scarf. And suddenly, in the mirror I saw Oscar.

He was lying at the bottom of the stairs, watching me, in an attitude of the most poignant allurement. His front paws were dangling over his chest, his eyes were swimming with emotion, and now and then his tail did a little twitch.

I stopped fiddling with my scarf, and stared at Oscar's reflection. The house was very silent. Then Oscar spoke. And this is what he said:

'Must you go out? Have you thought of *me?* When you have gone, when the front door has slammed and when the sound of your motor car has echoed into the distance, what shall I do? It is too cold to walk in the garden. I cannot stare at one of those strange bundles with fluttering pages which you call "books". There are no mice in the wainscot; those were disposed of years ago. You suggest that I might take a bath? But I have washed myself till my tongue aches. Or that I might go to sleep? But I have slept till I am weary of sleeping.

'So what shall I do? If I were in the jungle, where I really belong, there would be lots to do. Lots that I should *have* to do. I should have to hunt for food, and search for shelter; I might even have to fight for my life. Which would be very painful and exhausting, but at least it would be *living.* But you have relieved me of all those necessities; you have given me a home, and comfort, and two meals a day, and you have breathed something of your spirit into me. As a result, I am no longer a cat, pure and simple; I am to some extent a human being, with some of your own feelings and some of your own pleasures . . . and many of your ennuis.

'So please tell me, what shall I *do?*'

That is what Oscar is saying, as he lies there, glancing from me to the door, and making these small gestures of entreaty. And I hope nobody will suggest that it is foolish to endow animals with the power of speech. They *do* speak, to those who they think will understand. Sometimes what they are saying makes very painful hearing.

So what do I do myself, in these circumstances? Obviously, I harden my heart, and go to the opera. But some of the pleasure has gone, as I think of that small creature, waiting in the hall. I wish I could have taken him with me.

And that starts a whole new line of thought.

If only I *could* take Oscar to the opera! He would, needless to say, outshine any other member of the audience. We would sit in the Royal Box and he would perch on the edge, in a small but exquisite diamanté cloak. And should Madame Callas have an off-night and sing a little sharp, Oscar would sit up and sing a little sharper. And the great audience would stare up to the box and there would be nudgings and whisperings and wild questionings. 'Who is that ravishing creature in the Royal Box? It cannot possibly be Princess Grace, because tonight she is opening something in Monte Carlo. It must certainly be *somebody* royal . . . such majesty, such grace, such condescension!' And Oscar, who would of course be aware of the sensation he was causing, would gently incline his head and give a flick to his diamanté tail.

If only I could take 'Four' as well!

In his case, the problem of solitude is even more acute because, as we have already seen, 'Four' is the Cat Who Does the Act, and when he is not receiving attention he does not merely look sad, like Oscar, he invests the occasion with the most poignant drama.

This is what happens. I sit at my desk, engaged in the daily pursuit of telling stories, which is not always as simple as it sounds. The scene is set; things are just beginning to get under way; people are moving and speaking naturally on the foolscap. Then there is a faint scratch on the door. I try to pretend that I do not hear it, but a moment later the scratch is repeated, not quite so faintly. There is nothing for it but to get up and open the door, hoping, as I do so, that this will be merely a brief interruption, a routine visit during 'Four's' morning tour of inspection.

But as soon as he stalks into the room I observe with dismay that this is to be no casual call. 'Four' is 'drenched'.[1] Everything proclaims it. The way he weaves round the waste-paper basket; the way his tail flicks; the curious ecstatic *vibrato* of his purr; the manner in which he rubs against my legs and regards me with liquid adoration.

Who could ignore such demonstrations? One cannot give him a swift pat and tell him to go away. Still less can one shoo him out and slam the door. The consequences of *that* would be too dreadful to contemplate! He would rush from the house in high drama, his green eyes lit with anguish, his fur—metaphorically—waving in the wind like widow's weeds. Though he would not actually clasp his paws to his bosom, his high level of dramatic technique would enable him to convey this effect. And for days on end the house and garden would become a place of feline reproach, with 'Four' crouching in the shadow of the woodpile, or curled on a cold shelf in the tool-shed . . . 'Four' in his role of the outcast, the unwanted.

The reader will observe that there is not quite the same poignancy about the loneliness of 'Four' as the loneliness of Oscar. ('Five', thank heavens, is reasonably self-contained.) But though there is always something ever so faintly 'ham' about 'Four's' public appearances, there is nothing bogus about his affection. When he visits me at these awkward hours in my study I see him as a little creature who has sought me out because, for the moment at least, I am the most important thing in his small world. He is telling me so, beyond any question, by the music of his purring, by the weaving of his small black body, by the light in his uplifted eyes. And what choice have I but to respond?

All the same, there have been many times in my life—and doubtless there will be many more—when I wished, most earnestly, that cats could read.

---

[1] 'Drenched' is an expression used by Fs to indicate a condition of deep affection, which is outwardly demonstrated by cats in the manner suggested above.

TELLY

All my cats are keen 'viewers'—rather a common word, I always think, but it seems to have come to stay.

'Four' and 'Five' patronize Gaskin's set, because Gaskin is rather grand about commercial television, and prefers to tune in to the B.B.C. 'Four' and 'Five' share his tastes; there are fewer Westerns on the B.B.C. and the bangs make them nervous.

A very soothing sight it is, of an evening, with 'Four' on Gaskin's lap and 'Five' stretched flat out on the table in the middle of the little room, his ears at the alert and his green eyes focused on the flickering screen. This position is revealing. We have already noted that owing to an unfortunate episode in his youth, 'Five' likes, whenever possible, to repose himself in strategic places, where he cannot be come upon unawares. And I am sure that he has chosen the eminence of the table because of a secret fear that some day one of the monsters of the screen—such as a crooner—might come to life, and burst through the frame, and roar at him. This is a fear to which I am subject myself. I would not at all mind if *some* of the pictures came to life—if, for example, the magic box were suddenly to break open during one of the African scenes, and discharge a glorious collection of antelopes and giraffes. But if this phenomenon were to occur at a moment when Miss Never Mind Who was singing one of her pop numbers, I should feel very differently. To find oneself face to face with a female crooner, roaring at one with her bared fangs, lashing her bespangled behind, would be a fate worse than death. And please do not tell me that female crooners cannot 'lash' their behinds. They can, and do, with immense profit to themselves.

Upstairs the scene is equally peaceful. I sit on the sofa, by a log fire, with Oscar as companion. At the beginning of the entertainment, he usually disposes himself on my knees, facing the set, in a Sphinx-like posture. Then, as the drama quickens, his front claws gradually emerge, and I have a sensation of walking through a bush of exceptionally thorny brambles. I bear this for as long as possible, for I know that it is not a sign of hostility but a token of deep regard; however, the time comes when he must be gently detached, and persuaded to lie by my side. If this is done firmly, and if it is accompanied by suitable expressions of regret, the transition is effected without embarrassment on either side.

I often wonder what animals actually *see* when they are watching the moving screen. Obviously, in the case of static pictures, their eyes do not register any connection between the photograph and the original. The royal corgis, should they happen to open the pages of the *Tatler*, would not yelp with joy at the sight of themselves arriving at Euston station, as they so often do; and 'Five', should he chance upon a picture of myself in a less exalted journal, would probably sit on it. Nor do statues interest them. I once had a rather sinister stork, in lead, which had been wished upon me by a charming old lady, now deceased. It was destined for the water-garden, and I felt obliged to put it there, to please her. It would not be so long before it was largely obscured by a cluster of *onoclea sensibilis*, and in the meantime it might amuse the cats. It did not amuse them at all. They spurned it; you would have thought they were deliberately cutting it. The stork is now in the gardens of a maternity hospital, striking terror into the hearts of the inmates.

Their swiftest response, of course, is to sound. At the barking of a dog they are immediately on the alert, and at the sound of birds calling — *real* birds — their tails begin to lash. They pay no heed to synthetic bird song. By this I mean the strange medleys of trills and twitters, preserved on gramophone records, which accompany so many of the more sentimental moments of television drama. The play is nearly over . . . the night is done and dawn is breaking. The hero and the heroine, once more united, stand at a window, arm in arm, staring with bright eyes at a new world. Cue for trills and twitters. Even if the action takes place in a New York penthouse these tearful scenes are invariably played against a positive bedlam of bird song, made up of bogus thrushes and plastic larks. If the

heroine happens also to be having a baby, the bird song is even more persistent, particularly if the baby is illegitimate, as it usually is. One would almost think that child-birth in the minds of television producers, was connected, in some obscure way, with ornithology.

We still have not answered the question of what cats actually *see*. I would give a great deal to know; cats' eyes are among the most beautiful and mysterious jewels of the animal kingdom, and if we could only look through them, though but for a few seconds, we should have a vision of another world. From the purely physical point of view I fancy they are somewhat short-sighted. Often, on summer afternoons, when I am sitting by the lily pond at the far end of the lawn, one of them will emerge from the porch in search of me, in order, no doubt, to give me the latest espionage report, or maybe to register some complaint about the cuisine.

And there he will stand on the terrace, staring around, and looking straight in my direction. But he does not seem to see me, and it is not until I call or clap my hands that he proceeds to walk in my direction. I need hardly say that he never runs. To run would be contrary to every precept of feline etiquette. Dogs may run towards their masters, never cats. They walk, with the utmost delicacy and deliberation, and as they draw near, they begin to make polite small-talk in the form of a series of soft mews, which is a form of social prelude to more serious conversation.

But though they may be physically short-sighted, and though when they watch the television they may not connect the visual image with the human personality, they *do* watch, keenly and closely. And sometimes I think that, for them, this is a form of artistic appreciation. Maybe they are seeing the dramas of the screen transmuted into abstract patterns, from which they gain the same pleasure as we might gain from an impressionist picture, in which familiar shapes are shown in musical groups of significant form.

Or am I on quite the wrong track? As they sit there, my three Sphinxes, are they in fact gazing towards horizons, infinitely distant, which my eyes will never scan?

UNDERSTANDING

I have always had the feeling that if 'Four', 'Five', and Oscar were to drink some magic potion which suddenly made them swell up to twenty times their natural size—till they were indeed as large as lions—there would be no cause for alarm. True, I should be faintly worried by the thought of the fish bill, and I should be obliged to make immediate arrangements for the enlargement of the cat-doors. I might also feel a momentary dismay at the thought of the amount of sheer physical energy which would have to be expended, in the future, on such diversions as tummy-rubbing, tail-pulling, and reversed whisker-stroking. The cats, remembering the techniques of the past, might find my efforts feeble and trifling.

Apart from these fleeting anxieties, there would be no qualms. The complete trust and confidence which had been established over the years would not be affected. Mutual understanding is not a matter of size.

In this conviction I am confirmed by the most remarkable animal book ever written—*Born Free*, by Joy Adamson. If ever medals were struck for outstanding Fness, Mrs Adamson would certainly merit the supreme award, for it was she who reared Elsa the lion cub, and gained her love, and kept it. Never, as far as I am aware, has there been such a miraculous marriage of two worlds, the animal and the human; and yet, perhaps it should not be called 'miraculous'; if we had faith and love enough, this would be the way things were naturally intended and ordained.

These pages are not designed for religious discussion, but in this context I may perhaps be forgiven for suggesting that when St Paul wrote of the faith that 'could remove mountains' he meant precisely what he said. It is merely a question of degree. I am among those who are fortunate enough to have seen the power of one man's thought acting on another man's body, acting instantly and physically, causing nerves and muscles to react in a way which would be totally impossible of their own volition. If faith can go so far, it can go infinitely further. It can direct not only the bodies of men but all the bodies in the animal kingdom. There are—quite literally—no limits to its power.

Faith is merely a facet of love—the love of God. If you had enough of it, you could walk into the cage of the fiercest lion and sleep by its side. Once again, it is a question of degree. Perhaps the caged lion is an unhappy example, for it has been surrounded since birth by human hatred and mockery, so that its eyes are clouded and its heart is hardened. But with a lion with whose mind you are in harmony, or indeed with any animal, you can speak with love and your love will be returned.

No sooner had I written those words than there was a mew at the door . . . Oscar's mew. Entering, he sat down, gazed up at me, and mewed again. He has about six basic mews, on which he plays many delicate variations. This was number 3, in D flat, which, being interpreted, meant: 'This is merely a social visit; I was passing, and I looked in to see how you were, and if you were working well.' To assure himself on this latter point he leapt on to the desk, and sniffed the manuscript. Then he leapt down again, and stalked out, tail erect.

I closed the door and went back to my desk. And then I saw that across the foolscap he had printed his signature of approval—three clearly defined prints of his four-padded paws. They were the prints of a domestic cat, yes. But they were also the prints of a jungle lion.

Before we leave this theme of 'Understanding', let us apply it to some practical purpose. Let us suppose that we are carrying a kitten round the garden for the first time, holding it closely in our arms, introducing it to the Great Outside. In order to perform this task successfully we must ourselves *become* kittens. Fs will of course understand this procedure, but non-Fs may suggest that it is (a) ridiculous and (b) impossible. We need not argue about whether it is ridiculous; it is certainly not impossible. Indeed, it is a most salutary exercise for any human being. The non-F might be interested in knowing how it is done. Here are the main outlines:

INSTRUCTIONS FOR TURNING ONESELF INTO A KITTEN

1. Refocus the eyes. This is partly a physical and partly a mental process. Physically it consists in throwing the head back and lowering the lids until the eyes are half closed. Mentally it means a quick Gulliver translation to the land of Brobdingnag, so that natural objects such as flowers and trees appear as the kitten sees them—the daffodils the size of poplars and the poplars the size of mountains.

2. Close the ears tightly for at least five minutes, at the same time keeping the eyes shut. This will sharpen the sense of hearing.

3. Blow the nose, rinse the nostrils in cold water, and take several deep sniffs of smelling salts. This will sharpen the sense of smell.

4. Make certain that you really *are* in Brobdingnag. There must be no half measures. It is no use keeping one foot, as it were, in this world. You must be so deeply in Brobdingnag that when you see a snowdrop you wonder if you would have the strength to saw through the stalk and hoist it over your shoulder to carry it home.

Having carried out these simple instructions you will be ready to carry the kitten round the garden. Naturally, since you are only a human being, and as such deficient in many of the finer animal senses, you will be at best a clumsy instrument. However, if you stay firmly in Brobdingnag, and if you keep your hand on the kitten's back as a sort of receiver through which to interpret its emotions, you should not do too badly.

VOICES

One of the sternest tests for those who wish to qualify as advanced Fs is that they should respond correctly to the sounds made by Siamese cats. Many Fs—they may otherwise be quite intelligent people, who would pass most of the tests, with the possible exception of reversed whisker-stroking—have faulty reactions in this important matter. They will say: 'Of course, I adore Siamese cats, but I do wish they wouldn't make that dreadful noise.'

Such an observation rules out, for ever, their chances of getting into the Alpha-plus class of Fness. The most they must ever hope for is an Alpha-minus, and even this would only be granted after a long course of correction.

For to the really advanced F the cry of the Siamese cat is one of the most beautiful sounds he can ever hear. In the whole symphony of nature there is only one sound with the same bitter-sweet timbre, and that is the cry of the seagull. Sometimes as I have sat on the cliffs of Land's End, watching the white patterns of their wings against the black seas below, listening to their voices echoing far and near, I have closed my eyes for a few moments and mentally transformed the seagulls into Siamese cats. What a paradise such a picture conjures up for the true F . . . what prospects of ineffable bliss! To find oneself in a world where the heavens were alive with flying pussies, swooping and wheeling above! To look up to the sky and see flocks of kittens scampering among the clouds . . . to look through the curtains as night falls and observe that the boughs of the old elm trees were no longer cluttered up with a lot of old rooks but weighed down under a vast, purring accumulation of beige fur, with hundreds of jewelled blue eyes twinkling in the dusk! It hardly bears thinking of.

But we were discussing voices. Why have we used the word 'voice' for this section, rather than the word 'mew'? Partly because many of the charming sounds made by cats bear no euphonic resemblance to a 'mew', still less to the ugly 'miaow' which is attributed to them by non-Fs. But mainly because a 'mew' is too often associated with sadness. When cats speak there is no reason to assume that they are saying something melancholy or making some complaint about life in general; indeed, the very reverse is often the case. For instance, Oscar greets me at least half a dozen times a day with a wide range of soft, husky sounds which are evidently signs of approval and affection, for they are accompanied by intermittent purrs, leg-weaving, and erect tail-waving, and while he makes them he gazes up at me with enormous liquid green eyes. I do not insult him by assuming that he is asking for another helping of fish; he is doing nothing of the sort; he is merely passing the time of day, inquiring after my mood, and making amiable small talk.

It is the same with 'Five', most of whose conversation is conducted while he is lying on his back, with his front paws dangling in front of him. 'Five' is perhaps a better listener than raconteur; he prefers that one should open the conversation, contenting himself with interjecting brief staccato comments when one pauses, which may be interpreted as 'Yes?' 'Indeed?' 'No!'

However, perhaps the most accomplished conversationalist is 'Four'. This is only to be expected, since he is the eldest, with the widest range of experience. He is, for example, the only cat of mine who has ever been lost.

And now that we have mentioned *that* appalling episode, which created a sensation in feline circles for a whole three days, perhaps I may be allowed to give my own theories about it, for the benefit of the future historian.

I have long had a suspicion, amounting almost to a certainty, that when 'Four' was lost it was all part of his Act. He was giving a supreme performance of his Role. Look at the facts, in case the data of this *cause célèbre* has momentarily slipped your memory. It happened at Merry Hall, in June. To be precise, on June 21st, which is the longest day in the year . . . and it certainly felt like it, by the time we all got to bed. There had been some argument about the fish; I have never been quite sure how it began, but Gaskin assures me that he did *not* begin it. However, it was enough to make 'Four' tap an impatient paw, and go into the first part of his act . . . dejection, terror, starvation, etc.

At this point, Cherry enters. Cherry is a very nice friend of Gaskin's, with grey hair, who makes—so we all understand—vast sums of money on the films playing distinguished diplomats. When he is not so employed he often comes down to sit in Gaskin's room and tell him stories of the great world which—judging by the hoarse peals of laughter echoing into my study—must sometimes be not a hundred miles removed from the knuckle.

Well, on this never-to-be-forgotten evening, Cherry suddenly suggested that he should take 'Four' for a walk, and carry him in his arms for a short way down the lane, in order to coax him out of his Role. And since Cherry is F to the tips of his elegant fingers, Gaskin gave permission.

So out went Cherry, and scooped up 'Four', who by this time was heavily draped in the deepest *crêpe*. And down the lane he went, holding 'Four' very firmly and expertly, murmuring reassurances. You would think that 'Four' would have been flattered, but no. 'Four' was rigid. He said to himself . . . 'I am an artist. I have my role to consider. I will not be coaxed and wheedled by Mr Cherry, however much money he may be making. Apart from that, I have put on all this *crêpe* and an extra amount of eye-shadow and it is *not* going to be wasted.' (Those, I am convinced, were his very words.)

With which, he leapt from Cherry's arms into the hedge and completely disappeared for three whole days. But completely. We were up all night, and the next day, and the next two nights. The police were alerted, notices were posted all over the village, and though it would be an exaggeration to say that traffic was diverted, there were several times when I was nearly run over by the local delivery vans. If you stand in a country lane for hours on end, tapping a tin plate, you eventually get into a sort of daze.

And then, quite suddenly, without a word of explanation, 'Four' walked in through the front door. He was quite calm, his fur was sleek and glossy, and though he was perhaps not quite so plump he showed no particular eagerness to be served with his fish. He looked almost the same as on the night of his disappearance, with one highly significant difference . . . he had abandoned his *crêpe* and removed his make-up. And in his eyes was a tell-tale gleam of triumph—the triumph of an artist who has given a supreme performance and has reduced the entire audience to tears.

What all this has got to do with Voices I do not know. But I felt it necessary to give my own version of this drama, which has long been a subject of controversy in F circles.

WINDOWS

A tragic waif presses his nose against the window of my study. It is a bitter afternoon in December, and the shades of night are falling fast. There is a flurry of snow in the air, and the first flake falls on the waif's nose. The waif puts up his poor little paw to wipe it off. He shakes off the snow, and stays there on the window-ledge shivering . . . staring into the brightly lit interior. His mouth opens in a mournful, silent mew.

It is all deeply moving. Like one of those Victorian illustrations to Dickensian novels, in which waifs, as such, seem to be permanently stationed outside the windows of the well-to-do in never-ceasing snow-storms, so that the plot may take its course.

The only fault with the picture is that it is completely bogus. For the name of the waif is Oscar. And Oscar is, at this moment, replete with a large whiting . . . which can scarcely have been digested . . . to say nothing of a bowl of milk, and various scraps of sweetbread from my own luncheon. Apart from that, there is a cat-door, just round the corner, waiting to welcome him. To say nothing of the window of the upstairs loo . . . the one that we must get the carpenter to see to, because the branches of the wistaria are making it difficult to close.

As if this were not enough, he has already been in and out of the door of the porch at least three times in the last ten minutes. He has entered the room, tail erect, marched to the porch, and mewed to go out. Sighing deeply, and wondering how I ever manage to write anything more sustained than a motto for a Christmas cracker, I have risen from my desk and opened the door. A chill blast has blown in, swelling out the curtains, and sweeping the carefully arranged Christmas cards from the mantelpiece. Oscar exits. I go back to my desk. A minute later, he is back on the outside window-ledge, in his deepest waif make-up, and his mouth is once more opening in that mute, heart-rending mew. It is quite maddening, and I could not enjoy it more. And of course, I let him in.

So perhaps this should have gone into a section on Teasing, for no other interpretation can explain Oscar's singular behaviour. He is a highly intelligent cat; he knows all about the loo window and the cat-door. Indeed, the mellow rusty creak of the cat-door, swinging to and fro throughout the day as he makes his mysterious exits and entrances, is one of the happier echoes in the quiet domestic symphony of my life.

If I ever had to make a sort of surrealist gramophone record giving a composite sound picture of my ideal existence (there would probably be a very small sale for it) the *motif* of the cat-door would constantly recur, in a brisk tempo. Then there would be many sustained passages on the wood wind, to interpret the evening breeze as it sighs through the copper beech. And the soft silver 'toot' of the kettle as it reaches the boil in the tiny cottage over the way, punctually every afternoon at five minutes past four. And the hail on the roof of the greenhouse when one has been caught inside it during an April shower. And the thud of apples on a sunparched lawn, and the rattle of walnuts on the roof of the tool-shed, and the petulant 'chuff-chuff' of the squirrels when one slaps one's hands in a futile effort to make them go away, so that one might have at any rate a few handfuls of one's own walnuts at Christmas. The rattle of the walnuts would be almost the only percussion in my modest symphony; there is quite enough percussion in the world without adding to it.

Indeed, I should be sparing even in my allotment of bird song. I should of course include the two linnets who always serenade each other across the lawn in June—one from the pear tree and the other from the apple; and I might make very effective use of the screech owls who sound their eerie calls at midnight just outside my bedroom window. They give one a most agreeable *frisson*, and encourage one to believe in witches and evil spirits, which is, I think, an excellent idea, because the man who does not believe in evil spirits is unlikely to believe in good ones. But I should soft-pedal the blackbirds, who can be extremely annoying when one is trying out a tune in C major and they chatter away just outside the window in a nagging D sharp.

'Outside the window'—the phrase reminds me of what I began to write about—windows and Oscar's wickedness in demanding that they should be opened for him. There is a very special window noise associated with Oscar which would certainly be included in my symphony . . . the sound of his paw scraping on the glass of my bedroom window round about 7.20 a.m., just after he has had his fish in the kitchen. Why he has to tell me about it, wafting affectionate breaths of whiting over my pillow, I do not know, and why he has to come over the roof to do it, and print large black paw marks on my sheets, I do not know either. But I do know that I should miss these little visits very much; I hope it will be many a day before I reach out a sleepy hand to feel the comfort of his furry body, and find only an empty sheet.

I wish that my windows could be always open, on to the jungles and the prairies, on to the mean city streets, so that there might be a perpetual coming and going, a never-ceasing leaping and purring and scrambling into my small abode. But I am afraid that Gaskin might object. Three cats and one bachelor, he has sometimes hinted, are enough. He must be growing old.

THE END

I hope that the reader will not be offended if I turn away from him, at this last moment, and address myself to the three small creatures who have been our companions throughout these pages.

I want to write them a letter. It is monstrous that one cannot write letters to one's cats. Often, when I have been abroad, I have wandered down some nice little winding street in a Mediterranean port, and paused at a kiosk to look at the picture postcards. And there I have seen some deliciously shiny ultramarine concoction showing a lot of tumbled houses, reeling up a hill, with my hotel on the top. And I have longed to buy it and post it to 'Five', scribbling . . .

Dear 'Five',

   X marks my bedroom and there is a very nice balcony which you would enjoy. The fish is very good, but rather bony. There are a great many cats who send their love. I am afraid that they are rather bony too. However, I am taking some of them out to dinner tonight, so I hope they will not be quite so thin tomorrow. I hope you are being a good cat, and looking after Gaskin. With much love and tell 'Four' and Oscar that I will be writing to them very soon.

B.N.

   That is the sort of postcard that I would like to write, but somehow it never got itself written. So now we will make amends.

Dear 'Four',
Dear 'Five',
Dear Oscar,

We have been together, now, for quite a number of years. To you, it must have seemed even longer than to me, for you are cats and I am only a man. And seven years in your life—so we are given to understand —are equal to only one in mine.

Which means that you, my dear 'Four', are nearly 98. And I do wish that you would sometimes remember it, and not go rushing up the pear tree like a stripling, in order to sit there, and dab at the blossom, and roll your eyes so coyly. I must remind you that the old lady who lives next door is only 82, and she would never dream of behaving in such a manner.

This is a letter of thanks—the sort of thanks that really do come 'from the bottom of my heart'. The non-F would probably say that no thanks were due; he would say that I had given you a good home, and

that was an end of it. I hope it is true that you have had a good home. But I do not have to be reminded that it has always been *my* home—I have dictated the moves, and settled the localities, without consulting you. True, I would have consulted you, had I been able. True, again, I have tried never to go to a place where you would be unhappy. Even during that dreadful year when the gods drove me mad, and chased me back to London, there was a large garden. The fact remains that you always had to follow where I led. One day, you would be happily wandering about in familiar territory, and the next you would suddenly find yourself shut in a basket, amid an uproar of frightening sounds and smells, and dragged away from your beloved trees and lawns. And when you stepped out of the basket, cramped and frightened, you always stepped into a new world. And you had to begin all over again.

Yet you never complained. You never looked at me reproachfully, asking me: 'What right have *you* to disrupt our lives like this? Who are *you* that you should assume these dictatorial powers?' Maybe you did not ask these questions because you sensed that it had not really been my fault; maybe you knew that I had not been acting wilfully but under those strange human compulsions, either of temperament or of circumstance, that so often compel men to tear up the roots of their own true happiness. I hope that this was how you felt about it; I hope too that the roots have been torn up for the last time.

I find it hard to imagine life without you, without any one of you. If 'Four' were not, as it were, standing in the wings, waiting to do his act —and you know, my dear 'Four', it often *is* an act—I should feel that the drama of life had lost much of its savour. The day must come, I know, when 'Four' will play his last role, and I think that my heart will then tell me that he is no longer acting. I shall look into his eyes and I shall know. I would rather not think about that. And anyway, it might be the other way round. Sometimes, I almost hope that is how it will be.

If I did not know that 'Five' was sitting on top of the kitchen table, so regularly, so confidently, twice a day, waiting for his fish, I should feel that the peaceful rhythm of life had gone awry. Needless to say, the rhythm of one's life is not always so 'peaceful'; one has one's share of travails and troubles and tribulations. But in the background of my mind there is a haven to which I can retreat, and it is a haven which the three of you have created for me. It is almost as though, in the stormiest of weathers, when the winds and the rains are at the height of their assaults, I had only to close my eyes and hear, in the distance, the gentle solace of a purr. Half past seven in the morning, rain or shine. Half past four in the afternoon, winter or summer. Wherever I may find myself, on land or sea, I have only to raise my wrist, and check the time, and hey presto . . . there is the vision of 'Five' before me, on the kitchen table. Waiting to be served. Sitting very erect, rather as Queen Mary used to sit. Paws slightly spread out, like a ballerina at the ready. Tail hanging over the edge, giving an occasional twitch. Green eyes wide open, regarding the proceedings with interest and—what is most important—with implicit trust.

It is wonderful to see that look in your eyes, my dear 'Five'. As a man, I am not too proud of my standing, in the eyes of you and your kind. I have a guilt complex, whenever I think of the way in which men have conducted themselves towards you. We are both the creatures of God; we just happened to be born in different kingdoms. My kingdom, materially, is the more powerful, and it has exercised its power with a brutality and a cynicism which no animal would employ. You use only one pair of claws, dear 'Five', to protect yourself. You do not invent machines with a million claws, to tear out the heart of humanity. But all this, perhaps, is a little beyond the compass of our discussion.

Let me therefore thank you, once again, for the peace you have given me. Seven thirty in the morning, four thirty in the afternoon. The clock of life ticks on, and there you sit, daintily, precisely, waiting to be served. With that look of trust in your eyes. It is a look which gives me infinite comfort. It tells me that I have paid back just a little bit of that debt that I owe, as a man, to the wild creatures of the world.

And Oscar? Here my pen begins to falter, which perhaps is just as well. For Oscar is an unashamed sentimentalist, and I am not all that tough myself. So that when he sits on my lap, and gazes up at me with swimming eyes, and works himself up into such a frenzy of emotion that he begins,

ever so faintly, to dribble, I feel sorely tempted to reciprocate. Not to the extent of actually dribbling, but at least to the extent of drooling in my mind.

How greatly impoverished would be the quiet domestic symphony without you, my very dear Oscar! How I should miss all those subtle sounds I associate with you! The sound of your paw on my bedroom window, demanding admittance. The sound of the blind running up as I prepare to let you in. The faint mew that comes from outside, as you sit on the ledge, in assumed pathos. The 'plonk' on the floor as you jump down—the feel of your cold, clean fur on the warm blankets as I clamber back to bed, and the loud rejoicing of your purr, that slowly dies down and blends into a symphony of sleep.

The conversation . . . so brief but so revealing. The small talk as you plod across the lawn towards me on a summer afternoon. Mew, mew, mew . . . purr . . . mew . . . purr . . . mew. The mild protest when you come to the door of my study—usually at four o'clock—to complain that your fish has not been put out. ('But no, Oscar, it is only four o'clock, and you know that tea-time is not till half past.') The bright 'good morning' when you leap on to my bed, for the second time, with the breakfast tray. And sometimes—very rarely, thank heavens—the small cry of distress that tells me something is wrong.

And of course, the rending sound of fabric being torn as you scratch an old armchair, either in an exuberance of high spirits or as a sharp sign that you are not being given proper attention. Long ago I abandoned any attempt to cure you of this habit, just as I also abandoned the attempt to trim your claws. A brief reflection convinced me that it was cruel to do so. I love beautiful furniture, but the living must take precedence over the dead. People who put their Chippendale before their cats do not deserve to have either. As for the misguided young persons who have been hypnotized into buying modern furniture, those revolting objects, like surgical instruments, that are an offence to the eye and a menace to the behind . . . such people should go on their knees and pray for an immediate onslaught of the sharpest-clawed felines to tear the horrid stuff to pieces.

But we were talking of the sounds that I associate with you, my dear Oscar. And so it is with your shifting shadows. They fall athwart the pattern of my life. Sharp and clear against the blind, as you demand entrance outside my window on a sunny morning. Dark and mysterious across the ceiling as you sit by the log fire in winter; they dance in time to the flickering flames, leaping, retreating, pouncing—as though you were chasing invisible mice. Perhaps the shadow I love most of all is thrown late of a summer evening, when the sun is sinking behind the hills, and when the dark pattern of trees, falling across the lawn, is monstrously elongated, as though in a distorting mirror. Then, as you walk towards me, you are followed by a strange, ghostly companion, with a tail ten feet long, and sometimes you pause and look round and stare at it . . . and for a moment I can almost imagine that once again you are a kitten, and that you will start to chase it. Well . . . you are no longer a kitten, and I am not growing any younger, so that these phantom pursuits can only be followed in the mind. But it is fun to think about, is it not, my dear Oscar? It has always been fun, and always will.

And so . . . 'thanks for the memory' . . . all three of you. As the result of our close and mystic companionship—for mystic indeed it is —we are all of us, I hope, a little happier and wiser than we should have been if our paths had not met. On my side, I can say that with my hand on my heart. I should feel very proud if you could say it too, in your separate ways, with your paws on your chests.